£20.16

Beauty Salon

Book 1

Jenny Dooley
Virginia Evans

Express Publishing

Table of Contents

owner

hairdresser

nail technician

makeup artist

colorist

Bella Salon

MEET THE TEAM
Collin / Michelle / Lynn / Frederico

Collin

Collin has fifteen years of experience as a **hairdresser** and **colorist**. He is now the proud **owner** of Bella Salon.

Michelle

Our friendly **receptionist** and **assistant** is also a part-time student. She studies massage therapy and plans to join us as a full-time **masseuse** in March.

Lynn

Lynn is our expert **nail technician**. She also teaches **budding beauticians** at SoHo Beauty college.

Frederico

Frederico is a new member on our team. He is a **makeup artist** with training in special-occasion and special-effects makeup. He also works as a **hair stylist**. Frederico comes to us from a top salon in Los Angeles. To be treated like a movie star, come and see Frederico!

receptionist   **assistant**   **masseuse**

Get ready!

❶ Before you read the passage, talk about these questions.

1 What different jobs do you find at a beauty salon?

2 What skills should beauty salon employees have?

Reading

❷ Read the information from a web page. Then, choose the correct answers.

1 What is the main topic of the text?
   A giving information about a team of hairdressers
   B welcoming the new members of the staff
   C introducing the staff of a beauty salon
   D giving information on finding a makeup artist

2 According to the web page, ___ is also an instructor.
   A Michelle   C Collin
   B Frederico   D Lynn

3 Team member, Frederico ___ .
   A is a makeup artist in the movie industry
   B applies makeup and does hair
   C trains people in special-occasion makeup
   D uses special-effects techniques when styling hair

Vocabulary

❸ Fill in the blanks with the correct words and phrases from the word bank.

WORD BANK

colorist   masseur
hairdresser   makeup artist

1 Collin's _____ thinks that the woman should change her hair from black to dark brown.

2 Janet is a very good _____ and knows how to make your face look young and fresh.

3 Brad wants an appointment with his _____ to relieve his tense neck muscles.

4 The young _____ made a mistake and cut her client's hair too short.

4 **Choose the sentence that uses the underlined part correctly.**

1 A A <u>receptionist</u> answers the phone and makes appointments at the salon.

B The <u>nail technician</u> gave Mrs. Williams a new hairstyle.

2 A A <u>hair stylist's</u> job is to apply makeup on clients before special events.

B Sadie is studying to be a <u>beautician</u> at a local college.

3 A Mrs. Baca's <u>assistant</u> helps her prepare the treatments.

B As the <u>owner</u> of the business, Cecilia's main job is to assist the hairstylist.

5 🎧 **Listen and read the web page again. What kind of students does Lynn teach at the beauty college?**

Listening

6 🎧 **Listen to a conversation between a receptionist and a client. Choose the correct answers.**

1 What is the conversation mainly about?

A how many staff are employed

B what month the receptionist started work

C the need to find new talent

D plans to hire a new hairdresser

2 What job will the receptionist probably have in the future?

A makeup artist

B hairdresser

C masseur

D nail technician

7 🎧 **Listen again and complete the conversation.**

Receptionist:	Welcome to Bella Salon. I'm Michelle, the **1** _____ .
Client:	Good **2** _____ . I'm Patty Moore.
Receptionist:	Is this your **3** _____ time here?
Client:	Err. Yes, it is.
Receptionist:	Well, let me tell you something about us. We're a small **4** _____ with a friendly professional staff.
Client:	Is there a **5** _____ here?
Receptionist:	Yes, our team includes two hairdressers. There's also a nail technician and a **6** _____ artist.
Client:	There's no masseur on the **7** _____ ?
Receptionist:	Not yet. But in March, I plan to join the team as a masseur when I've finished my training.

Speaking

8 **With a partner, act out the roles below based on Task 7. Then, switch roles.**

USE LANGUAGE SUCH AS:

Welcome to Bella Salon.

Is there a … here?

There's no … on the staff?

Student A: You are a client at the Bella Salon. Greet Student B, then ask about:

● the staff at the salon

Student B: You are a receptionist at Bella Salon. Welcome Student A to the salon, then:

● introduce yourself   ● answer his or her questions

Writing

9 **Imagine that you are a receptionist. Use the passage and the conversation from Task 8 to write a note about the number of staff in the salon and their duties/skills (100-120 words). Make sure to mention the following:**

● who is on the team at the salon

● who is planning to join the staff soon

5

perm

color

blowout

style

IN STYLE AT *Bella* Salon

The best full service beauty salon in town!

Whether you want your hair **permed**, **colored**, or **straightened**, our hairdressing team knows best. Just need a quick **cut** or **trim**? Bella Salon is the place for you. Treatments include a **shampoo** and **conditioning** massage. Your session always finishes with a **blowout** and **styling**.

Our high quality services don't stop with just hair treatments. How about professional **manicures** and **pedicures** by our qualified nail technician? Or try a relaxing **massage** and skin treatment.

At Bella Salon, we believe you deserve the best in beauty treatments. Call today to make an appointment or have a free consultation.

Get ready!

❶ Before you read the passage, talk about these questions.

1 What kind of services do beauty salons offer?
2 Why do salons typically offer more than one service?

Reading

❷ Read the advertisement from a magazine. Then, mark the following statements as true (T) or false (F).

1 __ Shampoos are the only hair treatments offered at the salon.
2 __ Clients can get nail treatments at the salon.
3 __ Styling is included in the trim service.

Vocabulary

❸ Read the sentence pair. Choose where the words best fit the blanks.

1 **conditioning / blowout**

Janelle's hair felt very soft after the _____ treatment.

To avoid leaving with wet hair, clients often ask for a _____ after a cut.

2 **perm / color**

Clients like to _____ their hair, when they start to see it is turning gray.

Kent gave the woman soft curls with a gentle _____ to change her whole look.

3 **manicure / styling**

Ursula goes regularly for a _____ so her nails look pretty.

Mrs. Wilson is coming into the salon at 3:00 for her weekly _____ .

4 **trim / shampoo**

Jason has a regular _____ to get all the dandruff out of his hair.

Susan's hair is too long, so she will ask the stylist for a _____ .

❹ Match the words (1-5) with the definitions (A-E).

1 __ straighten   4 __ cut
2 __ pedicure   5 __ full service beauty salon
3 __ massage

A a treatment for toenails and feet
B a service that involves applying pressure to the body
C a place that offers several types of beauty treatments
D to make the hair shorter
E to remove the curls from one's hair

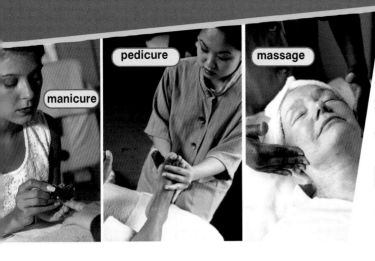

manicure

pedicure

massage

5 🎧 **Listen and read the advertisement from a magazine again. What does the salon offer at no cost?**

Listening

6 🎧 **Listen to a conversation between a receptionist and a client. Choose the correct answers.**

1 What is the conversation mainly about?
   A selling shampoo and other products
   B describing the services that are offered
   C booking a future appointment
   D finding out what services a client wants

2 What will the woman probably do next?
   A get a shampoo   C return later
   B have a haircut   D get a pedicure

7 🎧 **Listen again and complete the conversation.**

Receptionist:	Good morning, ma'am. How can I **1** _____ you?
Client:	I'd like a **2** _____ . Is there anyone who can see me now?
Receptionist:	Yes, Lynn is **3** _____ at the moment.
Client:	Great!
Receptionist:	Do you want any other **4** _____ while you're here?
Client:	What is there?
Receptionist:	**5** _____ _____ a manicure? Or you can get a massage afterwards.
Client:	Okay, I think I'll have a manicure.
Receptionist:	Fine. Your **6** _____ please?
Client:	Hannah Bell.

Speaking

8 **With a partner, act out the roles below based on Task 7. Then, switch roles.**

USE LANGUAGE SUCH AS:

I'd like a …

Do you want any other services while you're here?

How about …? Or you can get … afterwards.

Student A: You are a receptionist at the Bella Salon. Welcome Student B to the salon, then talk about:
● the salon worker that is available to help him or her
● whether he or she wants other services (suggest at least two services)

Student B: You are a client at the salon. Tell Student A what service you want and respond to his or her questions. Tell Student A what other services you want (if any).

Writing

9 **Imagine that you are a receptionist at a salon. Use the conversation from Task 8 to fill out the client information sheet.**

Bella **Salon**
Client Information Sheet

1 Name: <u>Hannah Bell</u>   Time: <u>10:30</u>
   Service(s): <u>Pedicure, manicure</u>
   Team member: <u>Lynn</u>
Notes: Client had a pedicure followed by a manicure.

2 Name: _____   Time: <u>11:30</u>
   Service(s): _____
   Team member: _____
   Notes: _____
   _____
   _____

3 Salon small talk

chat to

Get ready!

1 Before you read the passage, talk about these questions.

1 Which small talk subjects do you think are acceptable to talk about in a business environment?

2 Which subjects are NOT suitable to discuss with a business associate?

gossip

salary

hometown

marital status

The Dos and Don'ts
of Salon Small Talk in America

By: Sheila Ward

It's always nice to **chat to** your clients and learn about them. But remember, there are some topics that are **off-limits**. To make sure your clients are comfortable, never ask them about **touchy topics** like:

religion – politics – salary – marital status

What are some safe topics to **bring up**? Feel free to ask your clients about their **hometowns**, or how they **make a living**. Or ask about what type of music or movies your clients like. Some clients like to **gossip**, but make sure it's never about another client.

Beauty Salon Journal

Reading

2 Read the article from a magazine. Then, read the paraphrase. Fill in the blanks with the correct words and phrases from the word bank.

word BANK

money   job   off-limits   **married**   religious   favorite

Stylists enjoy talking to their clients, but they should not ask about topics that are **1** _____ . For example, do not ask about their **2** _____ or political beliefs. It's also not appropriate to ask about how much **3** _____ a client makes or whether the client is **4** _____ . However, there are plenty of topics that are fine to bring up, like the client's hometown, or their **5** _____ . It's also okay to ask about a client's **6** _____ music or movie.

Vocabulary

3 Write a word that is similar in meaning to the underlined part.

1 Megan often makes <u>conversation about non-serious topics</u> with her clients.
_ _ _ l _   _ a _ _

2 Kevin does not talk about subjects that are <u>not allowed</u>, so he doesn't make anyone uncomfortable.
_ f _ - _ i _ i _ s

3 Alison always <u>talks in a friendly, informal way</u> to a client while she's styling their hair.
_ _ a _   _ _

4 My daughter works as a manicurist to <u>make some money</u>.
_ _ _ e _   _ l _ _ _ _

④ Check (✓) the sentence that uses the underlined part correctly.

1 __ **A** Petra makes people feel comfortable because she talks about <u>touchy topics</u>.

__ **B** Oscar's parents still live in his <u>hometown</u>.

2 __ **A** Mandy did not <u>chat to</u> her stylist because she felt shy.

__ **B** Pablo earns a good <u>salary</u> each day as a colorist.

3 __ **A** Sammy often <u>gossips</u> about her favorite music in the salon.

__ **B** Ted's <u>marital status</u> changed when he got married.

⑤ 🎧 Listen and read the article from a magazine again. Is it acceptable to talk about other people's private lives?

Listening

⑥ 🎧 Listen to a conversation between a stylist and a client. Choose the correct answers.

1 What happens during the dialogue?

A the woman talks about missing her hometown

B the stylist complains about his salary

C the couple mention their travel plans

D the woman asks about a touchy subject

2 According to the conversation, what is true about the woman?

A She is a hairdresser.

B Her hometown is San Francisco.

C She travels often.

D Her office is close to the salon.

⑦ 🎧 Listen and complete the conversation.

Stylist:	Hello, ma'am. I'm Collin and I'm a **1** _____ here.
Client:	Hi, Collin. I'm Sylvia.
Stylist:	Nice to meet you. So, are you from **2** _____ here?
Client:	No, I'm **3** _____ San Francisco.
Stylist:	Oh, that's a great city!
Client:	It is, but it's expensive just like this salon. You must **4** _____ tons of money. What's your salary like?
Stylist:	I earn enough to **5** _____ _____ . Anyway, what do you do for a **6** _____ ?
Client:	I'm a travel agent.
Stylist:	Oh my cousin is a travel agent. He loves his job.

Speaking

⑧ With a partner, act out the roles below based on Task 7. Then, switch roles.

USE LANGUAGE SUCH AS:

Hello, ma'am. I'm … and I'm a … here.

So, are you from around here?

Anyway, what …

Student A: You are an employee at Bella Salon. Introduce yourself to Student B. When Student B asks you a touchy question, change the subject by asking him or her a question that is NOT off-limits.

Student B: You are a client. Ask Student A a touchy question about one of the following:

- what religion he or she is
- what his or her political beliefs are
- whether he or she is married
- how much money he or she makes

Writing

⑨ Imagine that you are a salon owner. Use the passage and the conversation from Task 8 to write a memo advising staff on how to make small talk with clients. Make sure to mention the following:

- appropriate topics to make small talk
- topics that are off-limits

4 Hair designers' tools

Get ready!

① Before you read the passage, talk about these questions.

1 What kinds of tools do hair designers use?
2 What is important to consider when buying heated styling tools?

wide tooth comb

cape

shears

Hermosa Beauty Co.   Beauty Supply Catalog

From **rollers** to **blow dryers**, Hermosa's Beauty Company has tools for all your hairstyling needs. Free **shipping** available on all purchases of $50 or more!

Cape	$20	**Unisex** hairdressing cape, high quality **water resistant**. Adjusts to fit all sizes.
Shears	$10	These top-of-the-line **stainless steel** shears are perfect for making clean and even cuts.
Clippers	$42	Give yourself the perfect trim with these high performance clippers. Includes mini **trimmer**, perfect for trimming **sideburns** and eyebrows.
Blow Dryer	$70	Gently dry your wet hair with this powerful (1875 watts) dryer. Six speed settings with easy to grip handle.
Curling Iron	$30	Curling hair is so easy with this quality iron. It heats hair quickly and evenly and comes with a long cord. And best of all, it's guaranteed not to snag!
Flat Iron	$50	Straighten **locks** with this **ceramic** iron. Unlike normal metal flat irons, our ceramic iron is guaranteed not to pull or break hair. Suitable for all hair lengths.
Rollers	$4	These comfortable rollers curl hair and prevent **tangles** and **breakage**.
Wide Tooth Comb	$2	A sturdy comb for untangling stubborn knots. This comb will help eliminate damage to fragile, wet hair.

Reading

② Read the excerpt from a beauty supply catalog. Then, choose the correct answers.

1 According to the catalog, which item is the best in its category?
   A cape
   B shears
   C blow dryer
   D curling iron

2 According to the catalog, what is true of metal flat irons?
   A They can break hair.
   B They are useful on damaged hair.
   C They work more quickly than ceramic ones.
   D They are less expensive than ceramic ones.

3 What is probably true about clients who order a blow dryer?
   A They have long hair.
   B They do not pay for shipping.
   C They receive a free catalog.
   D They own many beauty tools.

Vocabulary

③ Read the sentence and choose the right word.

1 Christina straightened her hair with a **curling iron / flat iron**.
2 The barber used a pair of **shears / rollers** to cut the boy's hair.
3 Kate used a **wide tooth comb / trimmer** to untangle her daughter's hair.
4 Jennifer bought a new **cape / blow dryer** to style her hair.
5 The beauty supply store sells **unisex / stainless steel** scissors that are small and easy to carry.

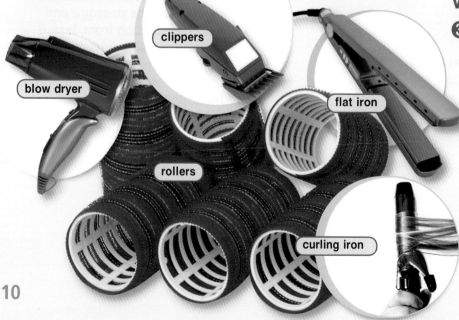

blow dryer

clippers

flat iron

rollers

curling iron

4 Place a check (✓) next to the response that answers the question.

1 Are there lots of tangles in your hair?
   __ **A** Yes, there are several knots in it.
   __ **B** No, my hair doesn't have curls in it.

2 Does this shampoo prevent breakage?
   __ **A** Yes, it keeps hair from being damaged.
   __ **B** Yes, it is guaranteed to stop hair growth.

3 How much is the shipping for these items?
   __ **A** It takes about 7-10 days.
   __ **B** It's free on large orders.

5 🎧 Listen and read the excerpt from a beauty supply catalog again. Which tool would someone use to make their hair straight?

Listening

6 🎧 Listen to a conversation between a sales representative and a hairdresser. Mark the following statements as true (T) or false (F).

1 __ The hairdresser is calling to ask about product prices.
2 __ The hairdresser needs a new flat iron.
3 __ The sales representative recommends a metal flat iron.

7 🎧 Listen again and complete the conversation.

Sales Representative:	Hello. You've reached Hermosa's Beauty Company. This is Tom. How can I help you?
Hairdresser:	Hello. This is Lisa Carter, I want to **1** _____ some supplies.
Sales Representative:	Of course, ma'am. What **2** _____ do you need?
Hairdresser:	I need a **3** _____ _____ _____ . I have a metal one now, but it damages certain hair types.
Sales Representative:	Well, we recommend using ceramic flat irons. They are less harsh on hair, especially **4** _____ hair.
Hairdresser:	Are they expensive?
Sales Representative:	Not at all. They're very **5** _____ _____ _____ _____ and we haven't had any complaints at all.
Hairdresser:	Really? Then I'll take **6** _____ _____ those, please.

Speaking

8 With a partner, act out the roles based on Task 7. Then, switch roles.

USE LANGUAGE SUCH AS:

I want to order some supplies.
What supplies do you need?
They're very good value for money.

Student A: You are a sales representative for Hermosa Beauty Company. Ask Student B questions to find out:
● the reason for his or her call
● what supplies he or she needs

Student B: You are a hairdresser. Answer Student A's questions.

Writing

9 Use the conversation from Task 8 to fill out the order form.

HERMOSA BEAUTY COMPANY
ORDER FORM

Client's Name: _____

Items Ordered:	Cost:
_____	_____
_____	_____
_____	_____

straight
wavy
curly
kinky/afro-textured
oily
frizzy/dry/coarse
volume
tangled
sleek

Metropolitan Woman Volume: 23 Issue: 6

What's Your Hair Type?

Take our brief quiz and find out!

Choose the correct answer:

1 Does your hair look …
   A brittle?   B healthy?   C greasy?

2 Does your hair …
   A break off when brushed?
   B fall into place easily?
   C need washing every day?

3 Does your hair …
   A look dull?   B feel soft?   C fall out?

If you chose mostly A's then your hair type is **DRY**.
If you chose mostly B's then your hair type is **NORMAL**.
If you chose mostly C's then your hair type is **OILY**.

Get ready!

❶ Before you read the passage, talk about these questions.

1 What are some different types of hair?

2 What kind of hair is the easiest/most difficult to work with? Why?

Reading

❷ Read the quiz from a magazine. Then, mark the following statements as true (T) or false (F).

1 __ The quiz helps people determine their hair type.

2 __ A person with lifeless, brittle hair has dry hair.

Vocabulary

❸ Check (✓) the sentence that uses the underlined part correctly.

1 __ A Cathy's <u>kinky</u> hair is easy to style because it has long and soft strands.

__ B Jane's hair feels greasy because she has <u>oily</u> hair.

2 __ A Alexis uses a flat iron to straighten her <u>curly</u> hair.

__ B Sarah's hair is uncontrollable because she has <u>normal</u> hair.

3 __ A Tara has to be careful with her <u>straight</u> hair because it grows in waves.

__ B Max has <u>dry</u> hair that doesn't have a lot of oil.

4 Write a word that is similar in meaning to the underlined part.

1 Beverly's hair is thick, full-bodied and has a lot of <u>quantity or amount</u>.   v _ _ u _ _

2 Rebecca's hairdresser uses a shampoo that makes her hair look <u>straight and shiny</u>.   s _ _ _ k

3 Stephanie's hair is <u>very rough and is difficult to comb</u>.   c _ a _ _ _

4 Jennifer's hair is <u>made up of strands that bend and look like waves</u>.   _ a _ y

5 Helen uses lots of hair products to control her <u>very curly and messy</u> hair.   _ r _ z _ y

5 🎧 Listen and read the quiz from a magazine again. What hair type is oily?

Listening

6 🎧 Listen to a conversation between a receptionist and a client. Choose the correct answers.

1 What is the dialogue mostly about?
 A the disadvantages of having curly hair
 B hairstyles for people with problem hair
 C treatments for dry, damaged hair
 D the problems with a client's hair

2 What will the client most likely do next?
 A cancel an appointment that was made earlier
 B ask the receptionist about her treatment
 C select a time to visit the salon
 D speak to a stylist about her dry hair

7 🎧 Listen again and complete the conversation.

Receptionist:	Thank you for calling the Bella Salon. How can I help you?
Client:	Hi. I'd like some **1** _____ about my curly hair?
Receptionist:	Okay. What seems to be the **2** _____?
Client:	Well, lately my hair **3** _____ when I brush it.
Receptionist:	Does your hair feel brittle or look dull?
Client:	Yes, it does.
Receptionist:	It **4** _____ like you may have dry hair. But don't worry. If you'd like to **5** _____ _____ the salon, we can give you a better opinion and some **6** _____ . Do you want to make an appointment?
Client:	Yes, for sometime next week. My name's Nancy Allen.

Speaking

8 With a partner, act out the roles below based on Task 7. Then, switch roles.

USE LANGUAGE SUCH AS:

I'd like some advice about ...

Well, lately ...

Does your hair feel ... or ...?

Student A: You are a receptionist at Bella Salon. Ask Student B questions to find out:
● the purpose of his or her call
● what type of hair he or she has

Student B: You are a client calling a salon. Answer Student A's questions

Writing

9 Use the conversation from Task 8 to fill out the consultation form.

Bella Salon Consultation Form

Client's Name: _____

Hair Type: _____

Problem: The client's hair _____ when it is brushed. The client's hair feels _____

Diagnosis: The client has _____ hair.

13

bob

chin-length

paneling

layers

page boy

shoulder-length

bangs

updo

Get ready!

❶ Before you read the passage, talk about these questions.

1 What kinds of hairstyles do women have?

2 What kind of hairstyle do you believe suits you the most?

Reading

❷ Read the article from a magazine. Then, choose the correct answers.

1 What is the article mostly about?
   A the best hairstyle for the office
   B different types of hairstyles
   C why some hairstyles are better than others
   D suggested hairstyles for special events

2 According to the article, how are the bob and the page boy similar?
   A Both styles come to the shoulder.
   B They look the same from the front.
   C Both styles are time savers.
   D They are not expensive to maintain.

3 According to the passage, which of the following is the best hairstyle for special occasions?
   A the page boy   B the bob
   C the updo   D paneling

Metropolitan Woman
Volume: 24
Issue: 4

Up or Down?

Discovering Your Perfect Hairstyle

Having trouble deciding on a hairstyle? Try one of these hairstyles the next time you visit the salon.

The Bob

The **chin-length** bob can save you time and money. It's great for the busy professional woman and never goes out of fashion.

Paneling

This edgy **look** makes **shoulder-length** hair fun and flirty. It suits someone with fine hair and increases volume.

Layers

Whether you have long or short hair, adding layers can create a stunning look and **revamp** an old style into something **sleek**.

The Page Boy

Let your **bangs** hang down with this classic **hairdo**! Getting ready in the morning will be quick and easy with this short **sassy** style.

The Updo

This hairstyle can add a touch of glamour to your look. It's perfect for special events where you may need a more formal style.

Vocabulary

❸ Match the words (1-7) with the definitions (A-G).

1 __ bob   5 __ paneling
2 __ shoulder-length   6 __ chin-length
3 __ page boy   7 __ layers
4 __ hairdo

A a haircut that emphasizes different layers or colors of hair

B hangs down to a person's shoulders

C a haircut in which some parts of the hair are cut short and others are left long

D a short haircut that is chin-length with bangs

E another word for hairstyle

F a haircut in which the hair hangs below the ears and curls

G hangs down to a person's chin

4 **Choose the word that is closest in meaning to the underlined part.**

1 The hairstylist trimmed the client's <u>hair that covers the forehead</u>.

   A layers   **B** bangs   **C** paneling

2 The magazine article recommends the <u>hairstyle in which hair is placed high on top of the head</u> for weddings.

   A the updo   **B** the bob   **C** the page boy

3 Susan wears a lot of makeup to enhance her <u>appearance</u>.

   A hairdo   **B** bangs   **C** look

5 🎧 **Listen and read the article from a magazine again. Which hairstyle would someone consider, if they wanted to improve and update their hairstyle?**

Listening

6 🎧 **Listen to a conversation between a stylist and a client. Mark the following statements as true (T) or false (F).**

1 ___ The stylist asks the client about her occupation.

2 ___ The client keeps in good shape.

3 ___ The stylist recommends an updo style.

7 🎧 **Listen again and complete the conversation.**

Stylist: How would you like your hair cut today, Miss Clemens?

Client: I don't know. What do you **1** _____?

Stylist: Why don't you tell me about your **2** _____? That makes it easy to decide which style is best for you.

Client: Well, I **3** _____ a lot. So, a style that keeps my hair out of my face is good.

Stylist: I know! How about a **4** _____? It's ideal for your active lifestyle.

Client: Is it **5** _____-_____?

Stylist: Yes, it's very easy to **6** _____ _____ _____.

Client: Well then, it sounds perfect for me!

Speaking

8 **With a partner, act out the roles below based on Task 7. Then, switch roles.**

Student A: You are a client at Bella Salon and you want to try a new hairstyle. Talk to Student B about:

● your lifestyle

● what haircut he or she suggests for you

● how difficult it is to care for the new haircut

Student B: You are a stylist at the Bella Salon. Talk to Student A and suggest the best haircut for them, taking into account their lifestyle.

Writing

9 **Use the passage and the conversation from Task 8 and the article to fill out the sign-in sheet.**

Bella **Salon**
Sign-In Sheet

Client's Name: _____

Hairstyle Request: _____

Stylist Suggestion: _____

Notes: _____

_____

7 Men's hair styles

Get ready!

1 Before you read the passage, talk about these questions.

1 What hair styles are common for men?

2 What is your favorite/least favorite hairstyle for men?

spiked
side part
long hair
crew cut
fringe
afro
buzz cut

Reading

2 Read the article from a men's style book. Then, choose the correct answers.

1 What is the main idea of the passage?

A how different haircuts show a person's character

B advice on styling men's hair

C how men's hair can make them look stronger

D examples of ways to style long hair

2 Stylists use clippers without a comb in order to achieve what effect?

A a side part   B a very short haircut

C textured hair   D tangle-free styles

3 According to the passage, what can we guess about long hair?

A It is more popular than short hair.

B It is inexpensive to properly maintain.

C It appears shinier than shorter hair.

D It can be hard to comb through.

What Your Haircut Says about you

Your hair sends an important message about your personality. What does your hair say about you?

Short cuts

Buzz and **crew** cuts which are very similar show that a man is active and strong. To achieve this look, ask your stylist to use a short clipper length, such as a one. For an almost shaved look, use the **clippers** without a **comb**. **Spiked** hairstyles, on short hair can look stylish.

Medium cuts

For a **classic** and businesslike style, ask for a medium-length cut. Then, part the **fringe** from the **hairline** to the back to create a classic **side part**. To achieve a messy, **tousled** look and add **texture**, **finger-comb** the hair and massage the ends with a little hair gel or wax.

Long hair

Long hair shows that a man is creative and passionate. Ask your stylist about the best products to keep your hair tangle-free and shiny.

Different hair

Hairstyles differ a lot between countries and are often related to various cultures, for example **afro-textured** hair which is often thick and curly.

Vocabulary

3 Read the sentence pair. Choose where the words best fit the blanks.

1 **fringe / hairline**

Sam's _____ is very short and doesn't cover his forehead.

The barber shaved Bob's _____ at the back so it was even.

2 **buzz cut / side part**

He chose a _____ because he's a soldier and needs a short style.

For many years, my father had a _____ before he eventually went bald.

3 **texture / crew cut**

A _____ is good for men who don't want to spend a lot of time styling their hair.

Kevin uses gel to add _____ to his hair.

4 **Write a word that is similar in meaning to the underlined part.**

1 The stylist cut his hair with <u>a device that trims men's hair</u>. _ l _ p p _ _ _

2 Sam doesn't like trendy styles, so he gets <u>traditional</u> haircuts. _ l _ _ s _ c

3 Jeri <u>uses her hands to tidy</u> her hair when she doesn't have a brush with her. f _ _ g e _ - c _ _ b _

5 🎧 **Listen and read the article from a men's style book again. How can someone achieve a tousled look to their hair?**

Listening

6 🎧 **Listen to a conversation between a client and a stylist. Choose the correct answers.**

1 What is the conversation mainly about?
   A trendy haircuts for men
   B why the man wants a buzz cut
   C suggestions for cutting the man's hair
   D how to properly use hair clippers

2 What does the man ask the stylist to do?
   A change his hairstyle
   B use the clippers without a comb
   C show him different men's hairstyles
   D give him advice for his long hair

7 🎧 **Listen again and complete the conversation.**

Stylist: So, Mr. Gonzales, do you want your usual **1**_____?

Client: No, I'm tired of **2**_____ _____. I want to try something different.

Stylist: What sort of **3**_____ do you want?

Client: I want it short on the **4**_____ and longer on top.

Stylist: Okay. Does a **5**_____ _____ sound good for the sides?

Client: Let's go a little shorter.

Stylist: How about a number 2? Then, I'll use a little gel to finger-comb it.

Client: Yes, that sounds good. Please don't take too much **6**_____ _____ _____, though.

Speaking

8 **With a partner, act out the roles below based on Task 7. Then, switch roles.**

USE LANGUAGE SUCH AS:

Do you want your usual haircut?

No, I'm tired of …

I want …

Student A: You are client and want a haircut. Tell Student B about:
● your desired hair length
● the kind of style that you want

Student B: You are the stylist. Respond to Student B's requests.

Writing

9 **Imagine that you are a hairdresser. Use the conversation from Task 8 to write a note to your employer giving him/her details about your last client. Make sure to mention the following:**

● what length the client requested
● how long he wanted it on top
● your suggestion for styling the hair.

Short notes regarding Mr. _____:

_____

_____

_____

_____

_____

_____

_____

_____

_____

8 Communicating during a haircut

Salon World Volume: 20

gown

communication

client

tilt

spray bottle

Making a Client Feel Comfortable

The secret to a great cut is **communication**. Use the following tips to communicate with your clients:

Before the Cut

Listen to your **client** to find out exactly what he or she wants. Show them a **style book** with examples of haircuts.

While You Cut

Give clear instructions. Ask clients to stand up and put on a **gown** to protect their clothes from **stray** hairs. Warn clients before using a **spray bottle** to **mist** their hair. During the cut, tell the clients when to **lean** forward or **tilt** their head. They will feel a lot happier if you explain to them what you are doing.

After the Cut

Let the client see the haircut. Ask questions to make sure the client is happy with the haircut. Remember, this is the last chance to make sure that he or she is satisfied!

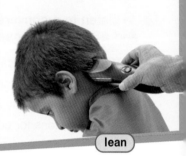

lean

Get ready!

❶ Before you read the passage, talk about these questions.

1   What is the best way for a stylist to communicate with a client?

2   What does a client usually expect from their hairstylist?

Reading

❷ Read the article from a magazine. Then, mark the following statements as true (T) or false (F).

1   __ A stylist should decide what hairstyle to give a customer.

2   __ Customers like it when a stylist tells them what they are doing.

3   __ A stylist should never ask if a customer is happy with their haircut.

Vocabulary

❸ Write a word that is similar in meaning to the underlined part.

1   Angela wears a <u>loose piece of material that protects her clothes</u> during her haircut.   _ o _ _

2   Jason <u>sprays a light layer of water on</u> the woman's hair in order to make it damp.   _ _ _ t s

3   The hairdresser found it difficult to get the young boy <u>to move</u> his head forward.   _ _ l _

❹ Check (✓) the sentence that uses the underlined part correctly.

1   __ A   Kelly <u>tilts</u> her head to the side, so the stylist can cut her hair.

     __ B   Peter protects his clothes with the <u>spray bottle</u>.

2   __ A   Gina wears a <u>gown</u> over her clothes at the salon.

     __ B   Lindsay has good <u>communication</u> skills and people have trouble understanding her.

3   __ A   Walter only reads the 'For Sale' advertisements in the hair <u>style book</u>.

     __ B   Gus found a few <u>stray hairs</u> on his jacket after his haircut.

⑤ 🎧 **Listen and read the article from a hairdresser's manual again. Why is it important to communicate with a client while cutting their hair?**

Listening

⑥ 🎧 **Listen to a conversation between a hairdresser and a client. Mark the following statements as true (T) or false (F).**

1 ___ The woman is visiting the salon for a trim.

2 ___ The hairdresser instructs the woman to tilt her head.

3 ___ The woman complains that the man takes too long.

⑦ 🎧 **Listen again and complete the conversation.**

Hairdresser:	Hi, Mrs. Clifford. Are you ready for your **1** _____?
Client:	I sure am. Remember, I just want you to **2** _____ _____ _____ .
Hairdresser:	Okay. I'll only take a little. Please lean **3** _____, so I can cut the hair at the back more easily.
Client:	Okay.
Hairdresser:	Now, **4** _____ your head slightly, this way towards me.
Client:	Remember, **5** _____ _____ _____ , I just want a trim.
Hairdresser:	I won't. That's great. You're **6** _____ _____ now.

Speaking

⑧ **With a partner, act out the roles below based on Task 7. Then, switch roles.**

USE LANGUAGE SUCH AS:

Remember, I just want you to …

Please lean … so I can …

Tilt your head …

Student A: You are a hairdresser at Bella Salon. Find out what type of cut Student B wants. Then, give Student B instructions during his or her haircut, being sure to mention:

● which way to lean

● which way to tilt his or her head

Student B: You are a client. Respond to Student B's instructions.

Writing

⑨ **Imagine that you are a hairdresser. Use the conversation from Task 8 to write a note about a recent client. Make sure to mention the following:**

● what instructions the client gave you about his or her cut

● how you made the client feel comfortable

Bella **Salon**

Notes About Clients

_____

_____

_____

_____

_____

_____

9 Manicure

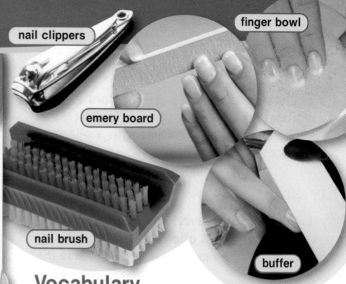

nail clippers
emery board
finger bowl
nail brush
buffer

A Guide to Your Nail Beauty Manicure

First, trim your nails to the desired length with the **nail clippers**. Use an **emery board** to **file** your nails. Be sure to move the file in one direction to avoid rough edges.

Second, fill a **finger bowl** with warm soapy water and **soak** hands. Use a **nail brush** to clean under and around the nails.

Third, rub **cuticle oil** on your cuticles to make them soft. Then, use an **orange stick** (not a metal cuticle pusher as these may damage fingernails) to push your **cuticles** back gently. Next, trim cuticles with a **cuticle trimmer**.

Finally, shine your nails with a **buffer** and massage hands with a moisturizing cream.

cuticle trimmer

Get ready!

① **Before you read the passage, talk about these questions.**

1 What different types of manicures do you know about?

2 What happens during a basic manicure?

Reading

② **Read the instructions from a manicure guide. Then, choose the correct answers.**

1 What is the purpose of the guide?

   A to give nail technicians advice on buying tools

   B to describe what tools are in a manicure set

   C to suggest different filing techniques

   D to explain the steps of a manicure

2 What advice does the guide give for avoiding rough nail edges?

   A use nail clippers to cut nails

   B soak hands in warm water first

   C file the nail in one direction only

   D trim the edges with a cuticle trimmer

3 Which of the following is NOT a step described in the guide?

   A put hands in warm water

   B clean the nails with a nailbrush

   C trim the nails with a cuticle trimmer

   D buff the nails to add shine

Vocabulary

❸ **Read the sentences and choose the correct meaning of the underlined word(s).**

1 Julissa used the <u>buffer</u> to polish her nails.

   A a container to soak your hands in

   B a device that cuts the skin around the nails

   C an object that makes nails shiny

2 The nail technician was careful not to cut too much of the <u>cuticle</u>.

   A a device that cuts around fingernails

   B skin around the nail

   C an object that makes the edges of nails smooth

3 Max cleaned the dirt from his nails with a <u>nail brush</u>.

   A an object with stiff pieces of plastic used to clean nails

   B a small piece of wood with pointy ends

   C a thin piece of cardboard used to shape nails

❹ **Fill in the blanks with the correct words and phrases from the word bank.**

WOrd BANK

> files   finger bowl   cuticle trimmer
> soaks   orange stick

1 Kate put her hands in the _____, which was full of soapy water.

2 A manicurist trims dead skin from around a client's nails with a(n) _____ .

3 After a long day at work, Max _____ his tired feet in warm water.

4 Penny often _____ the rough edges of her nails to keep them smooth.

5 Wendy showed her sister how to push back her cuticles with a(n) _____ .

⑤ 🎧 **Listen and read the instructions from a manicure guide again. What should you do to make sure your nails are smooth around the edges?**

Listening

⑥ 🎧 **Listen to a conversation between a student and a cosmetology teacher. Choose the correct answers.**

1 What is the main topic of the conversation?

   A discussing various tools for a manicure

   B giving advice about the best way to deal with cuticles

   C explaining the different uses of finger bowls

   D answering questions about something needed for a manicure

2 What will the teacher probably talk about next?

   A all the tools used in a manicure

   B additional manicure procedures

   C why cuticle care is important

   D techniques used by professional pedicurists

⑦ 🎧 **Listen again and complete the conversation.**

Student:	**1** _____ _____ , Miss Wilson?
Teacher:	Yes, Tina. Do you have a question?
Student:	Yes. It's about using the **2** _____ _____ . Do you ever add anything to the water in the finger bowl?
Teacher:	I usually add a **3** _____ _____ _____ .
Student:	There's one more thing. How long are you supposed to **4** _____ the fingers in the finger bowl?
Teacher:	**5** _____ question. You should only soak them for three to five minutes. Remember, you just want the cuticles to soften.
Student:	Oh, I **6** _____ . Thanks!
Teacher:	No problem. If there aren't any more questions, let's talk about other manicure techniques.

Speaking

⑧ **With a partner, act out the roles below based on Task 7. Then, switch roles.**

USE LANGUAGE SUCH AS:

Do you have a question?

Yes. It's about …

Oh, I understand now. Thanks!

> **Student A:** You are a student at SoHo Beauty College. Ask Student B two questions about having a manicure. Then, tell Student B if you understand his or her explanation.

> **Student B:** You are a teacher at SoHo Beauty College. Listen to Student A's questions about having a manicure. Then, respond to his or her questions.

Writing

⑨ **Imagine that you are a cosmetology instructor. Use the instructions and the conversation from Task 8 to write yourself a note about a question a student asked during class. Make sure to mention the following.**

- what the conversation was about
- what the student's questions were
- what answers you gave the student

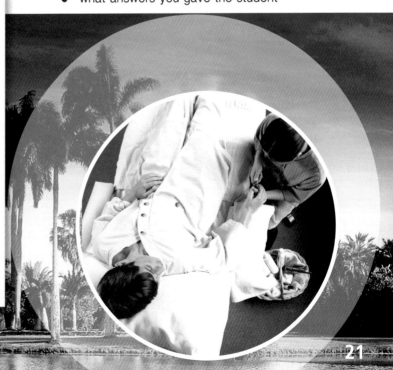

cuticle pusher

spa chair

foot massage

bowl

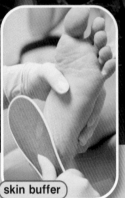
skin buffer

toe separator

nail polish

Bella Salon

PEDICURE SERVICES

What to Expect From Your Pedicure

- **What to bring:**
  a pair of **open-toed shoes** if the weather permits, a book or magazine to read

- **During the pedicure:**
  1 You are made comfortable in the **spa chair**.
  2 Your feet are soaked in a **bowl** filled with warm soapy water.
  3 A technician dries your feet and uses a **cuticle pusher** on your toe nails before trimming them. The technician also uses a **skin buffer** to remove any dead skin on the **soles** of the feet.
  4 The nail technician uses nail clippers and a **nail file** to cut and file your toenails.
  5 The technician removes **calluses** with a **pumice stone** and then massages your feet with a scented moisturizing cream.
  6 Finally, the technician separates your toes with a **toe separator** and applies a **nail polish** of your choice.

Get ready!

1 **Before you read the passage, talk about these questions.**

1 What is a pedicure good for?
2 What steps are involved in a pedicure?

Reading

2 **Read the excerpt from a salon's website Then, mark the following statements as true (T) or false (F).**

1 __ The technician trims the client's toenails before soaking the feet.

2 __ Calluses on the feet are removed with cuticle scissors.

3 __ The salon advises clients to take a pair of open-toed shoes to wear after their pedicures

Vocabulary

3 **Match the words (1-7) with the definitions (A-G).**

1 __ cuticle pusher
2 __ nail file
3 __ pumice stone
4 __ nail polish
5 __ spa chair
6 __ toe separator

A a small stone used to remove the hard pieces of skin on a person's feet

B an item that is inserted between a person's toes to spread them apart

C a thick liquid that colors finger and toenails

D a comfortable chair that people sit in while they have a manicure or pedicure

E a small tool that is used to push back the cuticles on a person's nails

F a metal tool that smooths the edges of nails

4 Write a word that is similar in meaning to the underlined part.

1 Joan used a pumice to remove the <u>thick or hardened skin</u> on the bottom of her foot.   c _ _ l _ _

2 Elizabeth wore a pair of <u>shoes that do not cover her toes</u> to the beach.   _ _ e _ - _ o _ _   s _ o _ _

3 Jennifer soaked her feet in a <u>large container filled with water</u> to relax.   b _ _ _

5 🎧 Listen and read the excerpt from a salon's website again. What do a pumice stone and a skin buffer have in common?

Listening

6 🎧 Listen to a conversation between a nail technician and a client. Choose the correct answers.

1 What is the conversation mostly about?
A complaining about a pedicure
B scheduling an appointment
C waiting to see a nail technician
D describing a pedicure to a client

2 What is true about the client?
A She is late for her appointment.
B She hasn't visited the salon before.
C She gets pedicures every week at the salon.
D She has already soaked her feet.

7 🎧 Listen again and complete the conversation.

Nail Technician:	Welcome to the Bella Salon! What can I do for you today?
Client:	Hi. I have a 3 o'clock **1** _____ for a pedicure. I'm Erin Fox.
Nail Technician:	Great! **2** _____ _____ _____ in the spa chair, Ms. Fox.
Client:	Okay. This is my first pedicure. Can you tell me what the **3** _____ is?
Nail Technician:	Well, first you'll soak your feet in some warm soapy water. Then, I'll fix your **4** _____ .
Client:	What happens after that?
Nail Technician:	I'll cut and **5** _____ your toenails, remove any hard skin and give you a **6** _____ foot massage.
Client:	Sounds great!

Speaking

8 With a partner, act out the roles below based on Task 7. Then, switch roles.

USE LANGUAGE SUCH AS:

Can you tell me what the procedure is?

First, you'll …

Then, I …

What happens after that?

Student A: You are the nail technician at Bella Salon. Talk to Student B about:
● whether he or she has an appointment
● the steps for a pedicure

Student B: You are a client. Answer Student B's questions and ask about the steps for a pedicure.

Writing

9 Use the conversation in Task 8 to fill out the appointment book entry.

Bella **Salon**

APPOINTMENT BOOK

Client's Name: _____

Appointment Time: _____

Service: _____

_____

Notes: _____

_____

_____

Contessa Cosmetics
Great New Items

Start your makeup routine with our new Flawless **Foundation**. Do you have **scars** or **blemishes**? Hide them with our Maximum Coverage **Concealer**. Then, apply our latest Earth **Face powder**.

To emphasize the natural beauty of your eyes, use our new Vivid **Eye shadows** and **Eye-Liners**. Make your eyelashes look longer and thicker with our Luxe **Mascara**.

Don't forget about your lips! Define your lips with our Tracer **Lip-liner**. Then, apply one of our new Always **Lipsticks** that stay on for hours. To add the finishing touch, our fruity **lip glosses** will add shine to your lips.

These items are sure to sell out fast, so visit your local cosmetics store today!

Labels: concealer, eye shadows, foundation/face powder, lipstick, lip-liners, eye-liners, mascara, lip gloss

Get ready!

1 Before you read the passage, talk about these questions.

1 Why do women like to wear makeup?
2 What kinds of makeup do people wear?

Reading

2 Read the website announcement about a company's new product line. Then, mark the following statements as true (T) or false (F).

1 __ A person with skin imperfections should use a concealer.
2 __ The new items are only available for purchase online.
3 __ An eye-liner adds length to a person's eye lashes.

Vocabulary

3 Read the sentence pair. Choose where the words best fit the blanks.

1 **blemishes / scar**

Elizabeth washes her face every night to prevent _____ .

Helga has a _____ on her cheek from an accident on her bike.

2 **eye shadow / lip-liner**

Before applying her lipstick, Kelly used a _____ to emphasize the edges of her mouth.

Sue applied a bright green _____ to her eyelids.

3 **lipstick / mascara**

That new _____ makes Audrey's eyelashes look very long.

Sara always leaves thick _____ around the edge of her glass.

4 **Write a word that is similar in meaning to the underlined part.**

1 Kate always has a difficult time finding a <u>skin colored liquid cream</u> that matches her skin tone.
f _ _ n _ _ t _ _ _

2 The sales assistant at the cosmetics store recommends using a <u>type of makeup that covers the flaws on a person's face</u> to hide skin imperfections. _ _ n _ e _ _ e _

3 The makeup artist carefully outlined the client's eyes with <u>a special kind of pencil used on the edges of eyelids</u>.
e _ _ - l _ n _ _

4 That cosmetics store sells a strawberry flavored <u>substance used on the lips to make them shine</u>. l _ _   _ _ _ s _

5 🎧 **Listen and read the website announcement about a company's new product line again. What would be the best way to hide unsightly spots?**

Listening

6 🎧 **Listen to a conversation between two makeup artists. Then, choose the correct answers.**

1 According to the dialogue, what is one of the benefits of using a Contessa's lipstick?

A It defines lips.   C It does not need re-applying.

B It tastes nice.   D It looks glossy.

2 Which of the following products is NOT mentioned in the dialogue?

A lip gloss   C lipstick

B concealer   D foundation

7 🎧 **Listen again and complete the conversation.**

Makeup Artist 1:	Hi, Alex. I **1** _____ _____ Contessa Cosmetic's fall line is now available.
Makeup Artist 2:	Really? I love Contessa's products. They're so glamorous!
Makeup Artist 1:	Me, too. Which product is your **2** _____?
Makeup Artist 2:	Hmm… It's so hard to **3** _____ . My clients love their smooth **4** _____ and fruity lip glosses.
Makeup Artist 1:	My favorite is their bright **5** _____ .
Makeup Artist 2:	What do you like about them?
Makeup Artist 1:	They **6** _____ _____ all day.
Makeup Artist 2:	Really? I'll take a look when I'm next in town.

Speaking

8 **With a partner, act out the roles below based on Task 7. Then, switch roles.**

USE LANGUAGE SUCH AS:

I hear that …

Which product is your favorite?

My favorite is …

Student A: You are a makeup artist. Ask Student B questions to find out:
- which product is his or her favorite
- why this product is his or her favorite

Student B: You are also a makeup artist. Answer Student A's questions.

Writing

9 **Use the website and the conversation in Task 8 and the passage to fill out the advertisement.**

Contessa Cosmetics

New Items on Sale!

Visit your local cosmetics store and buy one of these great new items!

Item:	Use:
Satin Foundation	Enhances your complexion
Liquid Eye-Liner	Emphasizes your eyes
_____	_____
_____	_____
_____	_____
_____	_____
_____	_____

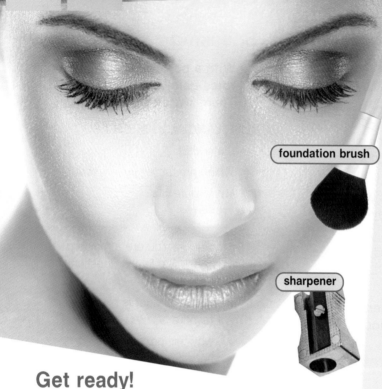

foundation brush

sharpener

Dear Mrs. Johnson,
Thank you for shopping with Hermosa's Beauty Company and for your continued loyalty. Based on your previous order, we think you might enjoy the following products from Hermosa's high quality range:

Mascara Wand - This wand is all you need to apply liquid mascara.

Eyelash Curler - For shaping and curling eyelashes and to make eyes look wider and brighter.

Brow and Eyelash Brush - This brush shapes unruly lashes and brows.

Foundation Brush - For a smooth, even coverage with liquid or cream foundations.

Lip Brush - For precise application of lipstick.

Shader Brush - For blending eye shadow.

Blush Brush - Great for applying blush or bronzer to cheeks.

Sharpener - A **sturdy** steel sharpener.

Cosmetic Wedges/Cotton Q-tips - Disposable tools for applying or removing makeup.

To order, please call: (1-800-232-8898)

Sincerely,
Davina Shaw,
Hermosa's Beauty Company

Get ready!

❶ Before you read the passage, talk about these questions.

1 What kinds of tools do people use to put on makeup?

2 How important is it to use makeup brushes?

Reading

❷ Read the letter from a beauty supply store to a client. Then, choose the correct answers.

1 What is the purpose of the letter?
   A to describe a problem with the previous order
   B to list the items of a recent sale
   C to recommend products to a client
   D to introduce special monthly sale items

2 Which of the following brushes is used to shape rather than blend?
   A lip brush   C shader brush
   B blush brush   D brow eyelash brush

3 What can you infer about Mrs. Johnson?
   A She is a frequent client of Hermosa's Beauty Company.
   B She always uses a lip brush to apply lipstick.
   C She has visited Hermosa's Beauty Salon.
   D She has never purchased a makeup tool before.

eyelash curler

brow and eyelash brush

mascara wand

Vocabulary

❸ Choose the word that is closest in meaning to the underlined part.

1 Alice used <u>a small tool to apply a product that colors your cheeks</u> to cover her cheeks with a golden bronzer.
   A cotton Q-tip   B blush brush
   C foundation brush

2 The makeup artist carefully applied the woman's eye shadow using a <u>brush that is used to apply makeup to a person's eyelids</u>.
   A shader brush   B foundation brush
   C blush brush

3 Jennifer used a <u>small, disposable sponge</u> to remove her makeup before going to bed.
   A sharpener   B cosmetic wedge
   C cotton Q-tip

4 Read the sentence and choose the correct word.

1 Our local pharmacy sells **lip brushes / cosmetic wedges** for applying shiny gloss.

2 Karen used a **sharpener / eyelash brush** to make her eye pencils more pointed.

3 Tammy always uses a **brow brush / eyelash curler** to emphasize her large eyes.

5 🎧 **Listen and read the letter from a beauty supply store to a client again. Which makeup tool would someone use to tidy up and smooth their eyebrows?**

Listening

6 🎧 **Listen to a conversation between two makeup artists. Mark the following statements as true (T) or false (F).**

1 __ The woman had looked in the cabinet for supplies.

2 __ The man tells the woman where to find the cosmetic wedges.

3 __ The woman needs a new sharpener.

7 Listen again and complete the conversation.

Makeup Artist 1:	Hey, Jenny. Do you need to order any **1** _____?
Makeup Artist 2:	Yes, I do need **2** _____ _____ _____ .
Makeup Artist 1:	**3** _____ _____?
Makeup Artist 2:	I could use a new **4** _____ _____ .
Makeup Artist 1:	Okay. Is there anything else?
Makeup Artist 2:	I also need some **5** _____ _____ , too.
Makeup Artist 1:	We have some of those. They're in the cabinet.
Makeup Artist 2:	Okay. Order me a new eyelash curler, so I have a **6** _____ one.

Speaking

8 With a partner, act out the roles below based on Task 7. Then, switch roles.

USE LANGUAGE SUCH AS:

Do you need to order any supplies?

I could use …

Is there anything else?

> **Student A:** You are a makeup artist. Ask Student B questions to find out:
> - what items need to be re-ordered

> **Student B:** You are a makeup artist. Answer Student A's questions.

Writing

9 Use the conversation in Task 8 to fill out the order form.

HERMOSA'S BEAUTY COMPANY
ORDER FORM

Employee's Name: _____

Item(s) Ordered: Quantity:

_____   _____

_____   _____

_____   _____

blush brush

cotton Q-tips

shader brush

lip brush

13 Makeovers

blush

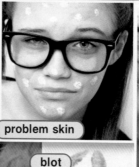

problem skin

makeover

blot

tinted moisturizer

clumping

Cosmetology Today · March · Volume 12

A Professional's Guide to Makeovers

By: Cecilia Barton, Gem Beauty School

Your clients trust you to make them look great. Follow these tips to give them the **makeovers** they want!

Always Start with **Cleansed** and Moisturized Skin
This helps **prime** the skin for makeup.

Determine Coverage
For **full coverage** (best for clients with **problem skin**), use a liquid or cream foundation. Use **medium coverage formulas** for clients with slight blemishes.

For **light coverage**, use a **tinted moisturizer**.

Other Tips
Use mascaras that reduce **clumping**. **Blot** the first layer of lipstick, so the second layer lasts longer. Only apply **blush** to the **apples of the cheek** to avoid a clownish look.

Get ready!

❶ **Before you read the passage, talk about these questions.**

1 Why does someone have a makeover?

2 What are some tips for a good makeover?

Reading

❷ **Read the excerpt from an article in a cosmetology magazine. Then, read the paraphrase of the excerpt. Fill in the blanks with the correct words from the word bank.**

determine	**layer**	**cleansed**
moisturized	**full**	**mascara**

Start with a skin that is **1** _____ and **2** _____ . Use a gentle facial cleanser and the correct cream for your skin type before a makeover. It is important to **3** _____ the coverage to apply the correct foundation. Coverage can range from light to **4** _____ . Other tips for a good makeover include using a **5** _____ that reduces clumping and blotting the first layer of lipstick to make the second **6** _____ last longer.

Vocabulary

❸ **Fill in the blanks with the correct words and phrases from the Word Bank.**

WORD BANK

tinted moisturizer   **primes**   **blush**
medium coverage   makeover

1 Lucinda uses a _____ foundation to cover a few spots on her face.

2 Polly's cheeks look bright because she uses _____ .

3 _____ moisturizer is perfect for light coverage.

4 Sheila looked completely different after her _____ .

5 Maxine _____ her skin by washing and cleansing it.

4 Read the sentence and choose the correct word.

1 Samantha finds it difficult to apply her blush across the **makeover / apples of her cheek**.

2 Maggie doesn't use mascara because it always **blots / clumps**.

3 Jack cleared up his **primed skin / problem skin** by using this face wash.

5 🎧 Listen and read the excerpt from an article in a cosmetology magazine again. What does it mean to prime the skin for makeup?

Listening

6 🎧 Listen to a conversation between a makeup artist and a client. Choose the correct answers.

1 What is the main topic of the conversation?
   A tips for makeup application
   B how to choose the correct coverage
   C the woman's skin problems
   D the advantages of full coverage foundations

2 What is true about the client?
   A She usually wears eye-liner.
   B She has problem skin.
   C She uses full coverage foundation at home.
   D She doesn't need powder.

7 Listen again and complete the conversation.

Makeup Artist:	Hi, I'm Mario, your makeup artist today.
Client:	Hi Mario. I'm Clara. I'm so excited about my makeover.
Makeup Artist:	Great! Let's start by putting on a **1** _____ _____, it will hide the redness on your cheeks.
Client:	Are you going to use a **2** _____ too?
Makeup Artist:	No, and you won't need any powder either. Your skin is clear and really **3** _____ - _____.
Client:	Okay. I certainly won't need any **4** _____.
Makeup Artist:	Now, **5** _____ _____ _____. As it's summer, I'm going to apply light blue and brown **6** _____ _____ today.

Speaking

8 With a partner, act out the roles below based on Task 7. Then, switch roles.

USE LANGUAGE SUCH AS:

Let's start by putting …
Are you going to use …
Your skin is …

Student A: You are a makeup artist at Bella Salon. Talk to Student B about:
• what type of coverage is best for his or her skin.
• what makeup you will be or won't be using

Student B: You are a client. Respond to Student A's instructions.

Writing

9 Imagine that you are a makeup artist. Use the passage and the conversation from Task 8 to write down a few suggestions for your client about doing her makeup at home. Make sure to mention the following:

• Suggest a level of coverage and makeup for your client
• Why your suggestions are best for her?

_____
_____
_____
_____
_____
_____
_____

14 Massage

shiatsu

deep-tissue massage

muscle

reflexology

scented oil

aromatherapy

Massage Services at *Bella* Salon
Experience the benefits of massage today!

Aromatherapy Massage
This massage combines **scented oils** and a variety of massage techniques. Choose from a number of aromas that either energize or relax.

Deep-Tissue Massage
Our masseurs slowly apply **pressure** to **muscles**. This massage relieves severe muscle pain and **tension**.

Shiatsu
This popular centuries-old technique improves mental health and **blood circulation.** The masseur uses his or her fingers or elbows to apply firm pressure throughout the body. This oriental technique releases energy from the body.

Reflexology
The masseur puts pressure on different areas of the feet. This massage also **stimulates** other body parts and helps relieve discomfort.

Get ready!

❶ Before you read the passage, talk about these questions.

1 Why do people get massages?
2 What are some benefits of a massage?

Reading

❷ Read the poster from a salon. Then, mark the following statements as true (T) or false (F).

1 ___ Deep-tissue massage gives people more energy.
2 ___ Shiatsu is an ancient technique.
3 ___ Reflexology involves massaging the feet.

Vocabulary

❸ Match the words (1-4) with the definitions (A-D).

1 ___ shiatsu   3 ___ aromatherapy
2 ___ blood circulation   4 ___ deep-tissue massage

A a form of massage that involves the use of scented oils in combination with massage techniques

B an old massage technique in which the masseur uses hands, fingers or elbows to apply pressure

C the transfer and movement of blood throughout the body.

D a form of massage that involves putting pressure on muscles in order to relieve muscle pain

❹ Check (✓) the sentence that uses the underlined part correctly.

1 ___ A James has large <u>muscles</u> because he exercises a lot.
   ___ B Amanda's hands feel better after her <u>reflexology</u> session.

2 ___ A Erica has muscle <u>tension</u> from having a long, relaxing weekend.
   ___ B Linda breathed in the sweet smell of the <u>scented oil</u>.

3 ___ A The masseur used oil in order to put <u>pressure</u> on the man's back.
   ___ B The relaxing massage <u>stimulates</u> other parts of the body.

⑤ 🎧 **Listen and read the poster from a salon again. Which massage(s) might you choose to increase your physical and mental strength?**

Listening

⑥ 🎧 **Listen to a conversation between a receptionist and a client. Choose the correct answers.**

1 What is the main topic of the conversation?

  A deciding on what type of massage to get

  B describing different scented oils and their uses

  C learning about the salon's aromatherapy service

  D changing an appointment with a masseur

2 What is NOT true about the client?

  A She chooses a foot massage.

  B It is her first massage.

  C She likes the scent of oils.

  D She wants to relax.

⑦ **Listen again and complete the conversation.**

Receptionist:	Welcome to Bella Salon, how can I help?
Client:	Good morning. I'd like a **1** _____, but it's my first time. What types are available?
Receptionist:	Our most popular is the **2** _____ _____.
Client:	Mmm … I'm not sure I'd like that.
Receptionist:	Oh. Do you need it for **3** _____ _____ or just to relax?
Client:	I just need to relax, I've been hiking all weekend. I don't like **4** _____ _____ though. Their scent is usually too strong.
Receptionist:	I'd recommend **5** _____ then. It's a stimulating foot massage, perfect for tired feet.
Client:	That sounds great!
Receptionist:	Okay. I'll **6** _____ a session for you.

Speaking

⑧ **With a partner, act out the roles below based on Task 8. Then, switch roles.**

I'd like a massage …

What types are available?

Do you need it for …?

> **Student A:** You are a client who wants a massage. Ask Student B questions about:
> - the types of massages available
> - why you want a massage

> **Student B:** You are the receptionist at Bella Salon. Respond to Student B's questions and help him or her schedule a massage.

Writing

⑨ **Imagine that you are a receptionist. Use the conversation from Task 8 to write a note about massage treatments available at your salon. Make sure to mention the following:**

- At least 2 different types of massages
- What the treatments help with

Bella Salon

MASSAGE TREATMENT NOTES

_____

_____

_____

_____

_____

clutter

massage table

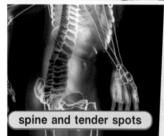
spine and tender spots

massage therapist

heel of the hand

Massage Basics

The Massage Area
Keep your **massage area** clean and free of **clutter**. After each session, make sure to **sanitize** the **massage table** and cover the table with the fresh towel.

Massage
Start by placing hands flat onto the sides of the body and spread out the fingers. Smoothly slide upward with some pressure. Apply pressure with the **heel of the hand** using the **Effleurage** technique, a relaxing soothing massage. To avoid causing the client discomfort, do not place pressure on the **spine**. Gently massage **knots** and **tender** spots to relieve tension.

Throughout the massage, ask the client for **feedback**. Stop immediately, if the client shows signs of aches or pain. Finally, remember as a **professional massage therapist** you should always make sure your clients are happy and at ease.

Get ready!

① Before you read the passage, talk about these questions.

1 What are the qualities of a good massage therapy clinic?

2 How do people prepare for a massage?

Reading

② Read the excerpt from a massage textbook. Then, choose the correct answers.

1 What is the main topic of the excerpt?
 A different kinds of massage
 B good places to give a massage
 C basic definitions of massage techniques
 D how to give a satisfying massage

2 Which is NOT advice that the excerpt gives about the massage area?
 A The massage area should be tidy.
 B The massage table should be covered throughout the massage.
 C A clean towel should be provided for each new client.
 D The massage table should be cleaned after every client.

3 What can we guess about the massage techniques described in the excerpt?
 A Professional training is required in order to use them.
 B They can cause pain if done incorrectly.
 C They cannot be performed without a massage table.
 D They focus on making clients feel energized.

Vocabulary

③ Read the sentence and choose the correct word.

1 Jason's boss likes him to keep his area neat and free of **feedback / clutter**.

2 Harriet asked the client to lay on her **heel of the hand / massage table**.

3 Jimmy **reported / sanitized** the broken spa chair to his manager.

4 Jane's back feels **tender / at ease** because she hurt it yesterday.

④ Read the sentence pair. Choose where the words best fit the blanks.

1 **knots/heel of her hand**

Rita rubs her client's backs with the _____ .

Samantha felt the _____ in the client's shoulders.

2 **feedback/Effleurage**

Eric calls his employer every morning to give her _____ about their clients.

Greg uses the _____ technique at the beginning of the massage.

3 **spine/clutter**

Wendy removes all the _____ from the room before her clients arrive.

Trevor is thinking about having a massage to relieve the pain in his _____ .

⑤ 🎧 Listen and read the excerpt from a masseur textbook again. During an Effleurage massage what should the masseur NOT do?

Listening

⑥ 🎧 Listen to a conversation between a masseur and a client. Mark the following statements as true (T) or false (F).

1 __ The client is having a foot massage.

2 __ The masseur causes the client some discomfort.

3 __ The masseur asks the client for feedback.

⑦ Listen again and complete the conversation.

Masseur:	Okay, sir, please lie down on the **1**_____ facing downwards.
Client:	Like this?
Masseur:	That's right. Now, tell me, where do you feel the most tension?
Client:	Mostly, here in my **2** _____ _____ .
Masseur:	Okay, I'm going to use the **3** _____ _____ _____ _____ to apply pressure.
Client:	Will that **4** _____ ?
Masseur:	It shouldn't do, but feel free to tell me. I don't want to cause you any **5** _____ .
Client:	No problem. I'm sure I'll **6** _____ _____ to it.

Speaking

⑧ With a partner, act out the roles below based on Task 7. Then, switch roles.

USE LANGUAGE SUCH AS:

Where do you feel the most tension?

Okay, I'm going to …

Will that hurt?

Student A: You are a masseur at Bella Salon. Talk to Student B about:

● how to lie down

● where he or she feels tension or pain

Student B: You are a client. Respond to Student A's questions and instructions.

Writing

⑨ Imagine that you are a massage instructor. Use the conversation from Task 8 to fill out these instructions to your students on giving a massage.

Giving a Back Massage

Instruct your client to:

_____

_____

Ask him or her:

_____

_____

Explain that:

_____

Glossary

afro [ADJ-U5, 7] When hair is **afro** (-textured), it has very tight curls all over the head.

apple of the cheek [N-COUNT-U13] The **apple of the cheek** is the fleshy area of the face. Blush is typically applied to these areas.

aromatherapy [N-UNCOUNT-U14] **Aromatherapy** is a form of massage that involves the use of scented oils in combination with massage techniques.

assistant [N-COUNT-U1] An **assistant** is someone who helps another person in his or her duties.

bangs [N-UNCOUNT-U6] **Bangs** are locks of hair that hang down over a person's forehead.

beautician [N-COUNT-U1] A **beautician** is someone who professionally styles hair and does makeup and nails.

blemish [N-COUNT-U11] A **blemish** is an unwanted mark on a person's skin.

blood circulation [N-UNCOUNT-U14] **Blood circulation** is the transfer and movement of blood throughout the body.

blot [V-I/T-U13] To **blot** something is to remove the top layer of something with an absorbent material.

blow dryer [N-COUNT-U4] A **blow dryer** is a tool that dries hair by blowing hot air on it.

blowout [N-COUNT-U2] A **blowout** is a professional hair drying service.

blush [N-UNCOUNT-U13] **Blush** is a cosmetic product that is often red, pink or brown and is applied to the cheeks.

blush brush [N-COUNT-U12] A **blush brush** is a small brush with soft bristles used to apply foundation or blush.

bob [N-UNCOUNT-U6] A **bob** is a short haircut that is chin-length with bangs hanging down over the forehead.

bowl [N-COUNT-U10] A **bowl** is a large container that holds water. It can be used for soaking a person's feet.

breakage [N-COUNT-U4] **Breakage** is a condition in which a part of a hair breaks off.

bring up [PHRASAL V-U3] To **bring up** something is to begin to talk about a subject.

brittle [ADJ-U5] If something is **brittle**, it is hard but easily broken.

brow and eyelash brush [N-COUNT-U12] A **brow and eyelash brush** is a brush with hard bristles that is used to smooth or shape a person's eyebrows or eyelashes.

budding [ADJ-U1] A **budding** artist, actress or writer etc is someone who is just starting their career and will probably be successful.

buffer [N-COUNT-U9] A **buffer** is a tool that makes nails look very shiny.

buzz cut [N-COUNT-U7] A **buzz cut** is where the hair is almost uniformly short all over.

callus [N-COUNT-U10] A **callus** is a thick or hardened part of the skin.

cape [N-COUNT-U4] A **cape** is a piece of clothing that covers clients in order to keep stray hairs off of them.

ceramic [ADJ-U4] If something is **ceramic**, it is made of clay or other materials similar to clay.

chat to [PHRASAL V-U3] To **chat to** someone is to start a conversation with them.

chin-length [ADJ-U6] A hairstyle that is **chin-length** hangs down to a person's chin.

classic [ADJ-U7] Something **classic** is timeless and not subject to fashion trends.

cleanse [V-T-U13] If you **cleanse** your skin, you thoroughly clean it.

client [N-COUNT-U8] A **client** is someone using the professional services of someone else.

clippers [N-COUNT-U4, 7] **Clippers** are an electric tool used to cut hair.

clump [V-I-U13] If something **clumps** together, like mascara, it forms lumps.

clutter [N-UNCOUNT-U15] **Clutter** is an untidy collection of objects.

coarse [ADJ-U5] If something is **coarse**, it is rough.

color [V-T-U2] To **color** hair is to change the color of the hair.

colorist [N-COUNT-U1] A **colorist** is someone who professionally colors people's hair.

comb [N-COUNT-U7] A **comb** is a device used on clippers to regulate hair length.

communication [N-UNCOUNT-U8] **Communication** is sharing information.

concealer [N-UNCOUNT-U11] A **concealer** is a type of makeup that is used to hide the flaws on a person's face.

conditioning [N-UNCOUNT-U2] **Conditioning** is a hair treatment in which a liquid or cream is applied to the hair in order to make the hair smoother and softer.

cosmetic wedge [N-COUNT-U12] A **cosmetic wedge** is a small, disposable sponge that can be used to apply or remove makeup.

cotton Q-tips [N-COUNT-U12] A **cotton Q-tip** is a small stick with a ball of cotton wool at each end which can be used to apply makeup.

crew cut [N-COUNT-U7] A **crew cut** is where the hair is short on the sides, but slightly longer on top.

curling iron [N-COUNT-U4] A **curling iron** is a piece of electrical equipment that creates heat and produces curls in hair.

curly [ADJ-U5] If hair is **curly**, it has a curved or spiral shape.

cut [N-COUNT-U2] A **cut** is a service in which hair is cut to a shorter length.

cuticle [N-COUNT-U9] A **cuticle** is the skin that grows around the base of the fingernail.

cuticle oil [N-COUNT-U9] **Cuticle oil** is an oil applied after a manicure to keep cuticles soft.

cuticle pusher [N-COUNT-U10] A **cuticle pusher** is a tool that is used to push back the cuticles on a person's nails.

cuticle trimmer [N-COUNT-U9] A **cuticle trimmer** cuts rough cuticles or hangnails.

deep-tissue massage [N-UNCOUNT-U14] A **Deep-Tissue massage** is a form of massage that involves putting pressure on muscles in order to relieve muscle pain.

dry [ADJ-U5] If hair is **dry**, it does not have a lot of oil and is damaged easily.

effleurage [N-UNCOUNT-U15] **Effleurage** is a massage technique that involves moving the palm of the hand in a circular stroking movement.

emery board [N-COUNT-U9] An **emery board** is a piece of cardboard with coarse emery paper glued to it. It is used for shaping and smoothing the edges of nails.

eye-liner [N-UNCOUNT-U11] An **eye-liner** is a special pencil that is used to emphasize the edges around a person's eyes.

eye shadow [N-UNCOUNT-U11] **Eye shadow** is a type of powder or cream that is used to add color to a person's upper eyelids.

eyelash curler [N-COUNT-U12] An **eyelash curler** is a tool that is used to curl a person's eyelashes.

face powder [N-UNCOUNT-U11] A **face powder** is a light, tinted powder used to cover any scars or blemishes or to give the face a less shiny look.

feedback [N-UNCOUNT-U15] **Feedback** is an opinion or information about a service or product.

file [V-T-U9] To **file** nails is to shape and smooth the edges with a special tool.

finger bowl [N-COUNT-U9] A **finger bowl** is a bowl in which the hands can be soaked before a manicure.

finger-comb [V PHRASE-U7] To **finger-comb** is to comb hair using the fingers.

flat iron [N-COUNT-U4] A **flat iron** is a tool made up of two flat metal pieces that produce heat. It is used to straighten hair.

foot massage [N-COUNT-U10] **Foot massage** is a massage technique in which one applies pressure to feet and toes for relaxation.

formula [N-COUNT-U13] A **formula** is a substance that is made by combining specific amounts of different ingredients.

foundation [N-UNCOUNT-U11] Foundation is a liquid or cream substance that matches a person's skin tone and is used to enhance a person's complexion.

foundation brush [N-COUNT-U12] A foundation brush is a brush that is used to apply makeup smoothy and evenly.

fringe [N-COUNT-U7] A fringe is the hair that hangs over the front of the head.

frizzy [ADJ-U5] If hair is frizzy, it is very curly and looks messy.

full coverage [N-COUNT-U13] A full coverage foundation is a cosmetic product that covers blemishes on skin.

full service beauty salon [N-COUNT-U2] A full service beauty salon is a place where several beauty treatments are offered.

gossip [N-UNCOUNT-U3] Gossip is a discussion about other people, sometimes about secret or unconfirmed details.

gown [N-COUNT-U8] A gown is a loose garment that covers the outer clothing during a haircut.

hair stylist [N-COUNT-U1] A hair stylist is someone who styles a person's hair.

hairdo [N-UNCOUNT-U6] A hairdo is a hairstyle.

hairdresser [N-COUNT-U1] A hairdresser is someone who cuts and styles hair.

hairline [N-COUNT-U7] The hairline is the area at the top of the face where hair starts growing.

heel of the hand [N-COUNT-U15] The heel of the hand is the hard, lower part of the hand that is right above the wrist.

hometown [N-COUNT-U3] A hometown is a the town where someone grew up or lives.

kinky [ADJ-U5] If hair is kinky, it has lots of small and tight coils.

knot [N-COUNT-U15] A knot is a muscle that is hard and tense.

layers [N-UNCOUNT-U6] Layers are a type of haircut in which some parts of a person's hair are cut short and others are left long.

lean [V-I-U8] To lean is to move the top part of the body towards a certain direction.

light coverage [N-UNCOUNT-U13] A light coverage foundation is a cosmetic product that is used on skin that is clear.

lip brush [N-COUNT-U12] A lip brush is a brush that is used to apply lipstick.

lip gloss [N-UNCOUNT-U11] Lip gloss is a clear or slightly colored substance that is used to give a person's lips a shiny appearance.

lip-liner [N-UNCOUNT-U11] A lip-liner is a makeup tool that is used to fill in areas along the outer edges of the lips with lipstick.

lipstick [N-UNCOUNT-U11] A lipstick is a colored substance in the form of a stick that is used to add color to a person's lips.

lock [N-COUNT-U4] A lock is a small number of hairs that grow and hang together.

long hair [N-PHR-UNCOUNT-U7] When hair is long, it is grown to a length longer than shoulder-length.

look [N-UNCOUNT-U6] A look is a person's appearance or style.

make a living [V PHRASE-U3] To make a living is to work for money.

makeover [N-COUNT-U13] A makeover is a process of changing someone's appearance through the application of makeup.

makeup artist [N-COUNT-U1] A makeup artist is someone who professionally applies makeup.

manicure [N-COUNT-U2] A manicure is a nail treatment in which a professional cleans, cuts, and sometimes paints a person's fingernails.

marital status [N PHRASE-U3] Someone's marital status indicates whether or not he or she is married.

mascara [N-UNCOUNT-U11] Mascara is a substance used as makeup to darken or lengthen a person's eyelashes.

mascara wand [N-COUNT-U12] A **mascara wand** is a tool that is used to apply mascara to a person's eyelashes.

massage [N-COUNT-U2] A **massage** is a service in which a professional applies pressure to muscles for relaxation.

massage area [N-COUNT-U15] A **massage area** is the area in a room or a room where the massage table is placed and massage therapy takes place.

massage table [N-COUNT-U15] A **massage table** is a table that is padded and has a special cradle for a person's head. It is designed to provide comfort and accessibility during a massage.

massage therapist [N-COUNT-U15] A **massage therapist** is a masseur or a masseuse.

masseur [N-COUNT-U1] A **masseur** is a person who gives massages.

masseuse [N-COUNT-U1] A **masseuse** is a woman who gives massages.

medium coverage [N-UNCOUNT-U13] A **medium coverage** foundation is a liquid or cream that hides small blemishes on skin.

mist [V-T-U8] To **mist** is to spray a fine cloud of water over something.

muscle [N-COUNT-U14] A **muscle** is tissue in the body that can contract and assists in movement.

nail brush [N-COUNT-U9] A **nail brush** is a brush used with soap and water to clean the nails.

nail clipper [N-COUNT-U9] A **nail clipper** is a tool used to cut nails shorter.

nail file [N-COUNT-U10] A **nail file** is a long tool made of wood or metal that is used to file a person's nails.

nail polish [N-COUNT-U10] A **nail polish** is a colored liquid that is applied on a person's nails.

nail technician [N-COUNT-U1] A **nail technician** is someone who gives manicures, pedicures and can apply nail extensions.

normal [ADJ-U5] If hair is **normal**, it has an average amount of oil in it.

off-limits [ADJ-U3] If a topic is **off-limits**, it is not okay or polite to talk about it.

oily [ADJ-U5] If hair is **oily**, it has a lot of oil and looks and feels greasy.

open-toed shoes [N-COUNT-U10] **Open-toed shoes** are shoes that do not cover a person's toes.

orange stick [N-COUNT-U9] An **orange stick** is a tool used to push back the cuticles on the nails.

owner [N-COUNT-U1] An **owner** is the person to whom something belongs.

page boy [N-UNCOUNT-U6] A **page boy** is a type of hairstyle in which a person's hair hangs below the ears and curls. Bangs hang down over the forehead.

paneling [N-UNCOUNT-U6] **Paneling** is a haircut that emphasizes different layers or colors of hair.

pedicure [N-COUNT-U2] A **pedicure** is a nail treatment in which a professional cleans, cuts and sometimes paints a person's toe nails. The treatment also includes massage and softening of the feet.

perm [V-T-U2] To **perm** hair is to treat hair in a way to set curls permanently.

politics [N-UNCOUNT-U3] **Politics** are the activities or ideas concerning the government of a country.

pressure [N-COUNT-U14] **Pressure** is physical force that is applied to a certain area.

prime [V-T-U13] To **prime** something is to prepare it before starting work on it.

problem skin [N-UNCOUNT-U13] **Problem skin** is skin that has many blemishes or marks.

professional [ADJ-U15] A **professional** is someone who practices a skill or a job which requires training and earns money from this practice.

pumice stone [N-COUNT-U10] A **pumice stone** is a small stone that is used to remove the calluses on a person's feet.

receptionist [N-COUNT-U1] A **receptionist** is someone who answers phones, greets visitors and initially deals with clients.

reflexology [N-UNCOUNT-U14] **Reflexology** is a form of massage that focuses on pressure points in the feet.

religion [N-UNCOUNT-U3] **Religion** is a belief in one or more gods.

revamp [V-T-U6] To **revamp** something is to change it in order to improve it and make it seem more modern.

roller [N-COUNT-U4] A **roller** is a metal or plastic cylinder that is used to curl hair.

salary [N-COUNT-U3] A **salary** is money received as payment from the company you work for, usually paid monthly.

sanitize [V-T-U15] To **sanitize** something is to make something clean and hygienic.

sassy [ADJ-U6] If something is described as **sassy**, such as hair, it means it gives a confident image.

scar [N-COUNT-U11] A **scar** is a mark that stays on a person's skin after a wound has healed.

scented oil [N-COUNT-U14] **Scented oil** is an oily liquid which has a smell. It is commonly used for certain types of massage, as well as in aromatherapy.

shader brush [N-COUNT-U12] A **shader brush** is a brush that is used to apply eye shadow to a person's upper eyelids.

shampoo [N-COUNT-U2] A **shampoo** is a service in which a professional washes a person's hair.

sharpener [N-COUNT-U12] A **sharpener** is a tool with a small blade that is used to sharpen the points of makeup pencils.

shears [N-UNCOUNT-U4] **Shears** are scissors that are used for cutting hair.

shiatsu [N-UNCOUNT-U14] **Shiatsu** is a form of massage that involves using the hands, fingers or elbows to apply pressure throughout the body.

shipping [N-UNCOUNT-U4] **Shipping** is the act of sending something, usually at a cost.

shoulder-length [ADJ-U6] A hairstyle that is **shoulder-length** hangs down to a person's shoulders.

sideburns [N-UNCOUNT-U4] A **sideburn** is the hair grown down both the sides of a man's face.

side part [N-COUNT-U7] For a **side part**, the hair is divided and combed to one side of the head.

skin buffer [N-COUNT-U10] A **skin buffer** is a tool used to remove excess or hard skin from ankles or the soles of the feet.

small talk [N PHRASE-U3] **Small talk** is simple and non-serious conversation.

sleek [ADJ-U5, 6] If something like hair is **sleek**, it is straight, shiny and healthy-looking.

soak [V-T-U9] To **soak** something is to put it completely into water and leave it for a while.

sole [N-COUNT-U10] The **sole** is the bottom surface of the foot.

spa chair [N-COUNT-U10] A **spa chair** is a comfortable chair that someone sits in while getting a manicure or a pedicure.

spiked [ADJ-U7] When hair is **spiked**, it is styled (often with hair gel) to stick up in sharp points.

spine [N-COUNT-U15] The **spine** is the series of bones running from the skull to the lower back.

spray bottle [N-COUNT-U8] A **spray bottle** is a container that is used to spray water.

stainless steel [N-UNCOUNT-U4] A **stainless steel** object is made from a type of steel that does not rust.

stimulate [V-T-U14] To **stimulate** something is to cause something to operate.

straight [ADJ-U5] If hair is **straight**, it has strands of hair that do not naturally bend or curl.

straighten [V-T-U2] To **straighten** hair is to make curly or wavy hair straight.

stray [ADJ-U8] If something is **stray**, it is not in its right place.

sturdy [ADJ-U12] If something is **sturdy**, it is strong, well-made and not easily broken.

style [V-T-U2] To **style** hair is to arrange a person's hair in a particular way.

style book [N-COUNT-U8] A **style book** is a book with examples of different hairstyles.

styling [N-UNCOUNT-U2] **Styling** is a service in which a professional arranges a person's hair in a particular way.

tangle [N-UNCOUNT-U4] A **tangle** is a knot made out of hair that is twisted together in an untidy way.

tangled [ADJ-U5] If hair is tangled, it is twisted together in an untidy way.

tender [ADJ-U15] If something is tender, it is sensitive to pain.

tender spot [N-COUNT-U15] A tender spot in your body is a part of it that is sensitive to pain.

tension [N-UNCOUNT-U14] Tension is the state of being pulled very tight and causing stiffness.

texture [N-UNCOUNT-U7] Texture is the way something feels.

tilt [V-I-U8] To tilt is to move part of your body, usually your head, slightly upwards and to one side.

tinted moisturizer [N-COUNT-U13] A tinted moisturizer is a cream that contains a little color and is used on people with clear skin.

toe separator [N-COUNT-U10] A toe separator is an item that is inserted between a person's toes to spread them apart.

touchy topic [N PHRASE-U3] A touchy topic is a subject that people are not comfortable talking about with strangers.

tousled [ADJ-U7] When hair is tousled, it looks untidy and uncombed but in an attractive way.

trim [N-COUNT-U2] A trim is a service in which the ends of the hair get cut off.

trimmer [N-COUNT-U4] A trimmer is an electric tool that cuts off the ends of hair.

unisex [ADJ-U4] If something is unisex, it is intended for both men and women.

updo [N-UNCOUNT-U6] An updo is a type of hairstyle in which a person's hair is placed high on top of their head.

volume [N-UNCOUNT-U5] Volume is the quantity or amount of something.

water resistant [ADJ-U4] Water resistant is something that cannot be damaged by water or water cannot pass through it.

wavy [ADJ-U5] If hair is wavy, it has strands of hair with curves that look like waves.

wide tooth comb [N-COUNT-U4] A wide tooth comb is an object with teeth along one side that is commonly used to untangle hair.

Career Paths

Beauty Salon

Book
2

Jenny Dooley

Virginia Evans

Express Publishing

Table of Contents

1 Busy day at the salon

waiting area

greet

sign-in sheet

Bella Salon Employee Manual

The Bella Salon's expert stylists and convenient location make it one of the busiest salons in the area. Follow these reception **guidelines** in the **rule book** to keep our clients satisfied even during **peak hours**.

- **Greet** all clients with a friendly smile.
- Does the client have an **appointment**? Remember, some services are available **by appointment only**. Tell a client with an appointment that a stylist will see him or her shortly.
- Many of our clients are **walk-ins**. Inform these clients of the **wait time**. During peak business hours the wait time can be over an hour, so make sure the client doesn't **mind** waiting to see a stylist.
- If they are prepared to wait, kindly ask these clients to write their names on the **sign-in sheet** and **direct** them to the **waiting area**.
- Offer waiting clients a cup of coffee or a magazine. Remember, a satisfied client is more likely to be a **repeat client**!

Get ready!

1 **Before you read the passage, talk about these questions.**

1 How can clients avoid wait times at a busy salon?

2 What should a receptionist do when a client arrives without an appointment?

Reading

2 **Read the excerpt from an employee manual. Then, choose the correct answers.**

1 What is the main topic of the manual?

   A how to schedule an appointment

   B advising employees what to do during busy times

   C describing the proper way to greet clients

   D telling employees how to use the sign-in sheet

2 According to the passage, why should the receptionist ask a client if he or she has an appointment?

   A Some services are only available to clients with appointments.

   B Stylists do not usually see clients without an appointment.

   C Only the receptionist schedules appointments.

   D The wait time is shorter for clients without an appointment.

3 Which of the following is NOT one of the receptionist's responsibilities?

   A informing clients of the wait time

   B welcoming clients to the salon

   C directing clients to the waiting area

   D writing names on the sign-in sheet

Vocabulary

3 **Match the words (1-6) with the definitions (A-F).**

1 __ guideline   4 __ appointment

2 __ wait time   5 __ walk-in

3 __ direct   6 __ greet

A a person who visits a business without making an appointment

B a rule describing the appropriate way to act in a specific situation

C an arrangement to meet someone at a specific time and location

D the length of time a person has to wait before he or she can see someone

E to show someone the way to a place

F to welcome someone when they arrive at a place

4 Check (✓) the sentence that uses the underlined part correctly.

1 __ **A** The hair salon offers haircuts <u>by appointment only</u>.

__ **B** The beauty store is empty during <u>peak hours</u>.

2 __ **A** David doesn't <u>mind</u> working late because he enjoys his job.

__ **B** The stylist colors clients' hair in the <u>waiting area</u>.

3 __ **A** John, a <u>repeat client</u>, visited the salon for the first time today.

__ **B** After entering the salon, Robert wrote his name on the <u>sign-in sheet</u>.

5 🎧 Listen and read the excerpt from a employee manual again. What must a client without an appointment do on arriving at the salon?

Listening

6 🎧 Listen to a conversation between a receptionist and a client. Mark the following statements as true (T) or false (F).

1 __ The client has an appointment to get his haircut.

2 __ The receptionist knows how long the wait will be.

3 __ The salon has magazines available for clients who are waiting.

7 🎧 Listen again and complete the conversation.

Receptionist:	Good afternoon and welcome to the Bella Salon!
Client:	Hello.
Receptionist:	Do you have **1** _____ _____?
Client:	Uh, no, I don't. I thought I'd just **2** _____ _____ for a quick trim.
Receptionist:	Oh, well, **3** _____ _____ is going to be about twenty minutes. Is that okay?
Client:	Sure, that's fine.
Receptionist:	Great! Please write your name on the **4** _____-_____ _____ . Then, you can have a seat in the **5** _____ _____ over there.
Client:	All right.
Receptionist:	Would you like anything to drink while you wait, some water, or coffee perhaps?
Client:	Oh, uh, no thanks. I'll just leaf through the magazines on the table.

Speaking

8 With a partner, act out the roles below based on Task 7. Then, switch roles.

USE LANGUAGE SUCH AS:

Do you have an appointment?

The wait time is going to be about …

Would you like anything to drink while you wait?

Student A: You are a receptionist at Bella Salon. Talk to Student B about:
- if he or she has an appointment
- the expected wait time
- if he or she wants a drink

Student B: You are a client. Answer Student A's question.

Writing

9 You are a salon owner. Use the excerpt and the conversation from Task 8 to write a section in an employee manual for receptionists. Make sure to mention the following:.

- Why you need to ask clients about appointments
- What you do if a client is a walk-in
- What you offer waiting clients

Receptionist Employee Manual

_____

_____

_____

_____

_____

_____

boulevard

freeway

landmark

Bella Salon

Location:

3278 Wilshire Blvd, Los Angeles, CA 90076

The Bella Salon is located on the first **floor** of the Wilshire Building. Nearby **landmarks** include the Royal Point Hotel and the Hancock Park.

Directions:

From Los Angeles International Airport:

1   **Go straight** toward the Airport Exit on World Way.

2   **Head** south on Sepulveda Boulevard toward the **Interstate** 105 **freeway** entrance.

3   Take the **ramp** onto Interstate 105.

4   **Merge** onto the Interstate 110 **exit** toward Los Angeles.

5   Take the 9th Street exit toward downtown.

6   **Turn** right onto Figueroa Street.

7   Turn left onto Wilshire **Boulevard**.

8   **Arrive** at 3278 Wilshire Boulevard. Your **destination** is on the right side of the street.

From Interstate 5 South:

1   Take the California 110 South exit toward Los Angeles.

2   Take the 6th Street exit onto Beaudry Avenue toward Wilshire Boulevard

3   Turn left onto Wilshire Boulevard. Your destination is on the right.

Get ready!

❶ Before you read the passage, talk about these questions.

1   What are some words you use when you give directions?

2   Are you able to give directions and follow them?

Reading

❷ Read the directions for the Bella Salon taken from their website. Then, mark the following statements as true (T) or false (F).

1   __ The Bella Salon is in the same building as a hotel.

2   __ Clients can travel to the salon on the freeway.

3   __ The salon can only be accessed from the airport.

Vocabulary

❸ Write a word that is similar in meaning to the underlined part.

1   Alexander arrived at his place that he was traveling to.
    d _ _ t _ n a _ i _ _

2   The store is located on the second level of the building.
    _ l _ _ r

3   Cheryl needs to travel in a straight line to reach Stephanie's house.   _ o   s _ _ a _ g _ _

4   The bus needs to change direction once it reaches Main Street.
    t _ _ n

❹ Choose the word that is closest in meaning to the underlined part.

1   The fastest way to reach the salon is to take the large road used for traveling fast across long distances.
    A entrance   **B** freeway   **C** exit

2   Emma used the city's well-known and easily recognizable buildings to find the hotel.
    A landmarks   **B** interstates   **C** ramps

3   Thomas traveled north along the freeway to reach his destination.
    A merged   **B** arrived   **C** headed

5 🎧 Listen and read the directions from a salon's website again. If you take the California 110 South exit, what must you do when you reach Wilshire Boulevard?

Listening

6 🎧 Listen to a conversation between a receptionist and a caller. Choose the correct answers.

1 What is the conversation mostly about?
   A the city that the salon is located in
   B which landmarks are near the salon
   C what routes to take to reach the salon
   D how to avoid traffic on the freeway

2 What can you infer about the caller?
   A She has a hard time remembering directions.
   B She has never been to the salon before.
   C She gets her haircut once every two months.
   D She doesn't like driving on the freeway.

7 🎧 Listen again and complete the conversation.

Receptionist:	Thank you for calling the Bella Salon. This is Ken. How can I help you?
Caller:	Hi. Can you 1 _____ _____ _____ to the salon?
Receptionist:	Sure. Where are you 2 _____ _____?
Caller:	Burbank.
Receptionist:	All right. First, take the Interstate 5 freeway heading south.
Caller:	Okay. What do I do once I'm on the freeway?
Receptionist:	3 _____ _____ for about 5 miles. Then, 4 _____ onto the Interstate 110 exit heading toward Los Angeles.
Caller:	Then, what?
Receptionist:	Take the 9th Street 5 _____ toward downtown.
Caller:	What do I do once I reach downtown?
Receptionist:	Make a left onto Wilshire Boulevard. The salon is on the 6 _____ _____ next to a hotel. You 7 _____ _____ _____ .
Caller:	Thanks for your help.

Speaking

8 With a partner, act out the roles below based on Task 7. Then, switch roles.

Student A: You are a receptionist at the Bella Salon. Give Student B directions to the salon. Be sure to mention:
● what freeway to take
● what streets to turn onto
● landmarks near the salon

Student B: You are a caller asking for directions to the Bella Salon. Respond to Student A's directions.

Writing

9 You are a salon receptionist. Use the website and the conversation from Task 8 to write directions for clients who want to visit your salon. Make sure to mention:

● Which freeway the client should take
● What street the client should turn onto
● What landmarks are near the salon

www.BellaSalon.com

summer look

salon staff

client

Bella Salon
Summer Hours

To Our **Esteemed** Clients:

The Bella Salon is happy to announce new **extended business hours** to give you all the opportunity to create a new **summer look**. We will now open earlier and close later in an effort to better **meet your needs**.

Our doors will open at 9 am and close at 8 pm every **weekday**. We will also be open bright and early every Saturday at 8 am. Sundays and **holidays** such as the New Year will continue to be **off days**. The new **hours of operation** are as follows:

Mondays	9:00 am to 8:00 pm
Tuesdays	9:00 am to 8:00 pm
Wednesdays	9:00 am to 8:00 pm
Thursdays	9:00 am to 8:00 pm
Fridays	9:00 am to 8:00 pm
Saturdays	8:00 am to 5:00 pm
Sundays	Closed
Holidays	Closed

The new hours will begin on Monday, June 2nd. **Regular business hours** will continue to be **in effect** until then.

We would like to express our **gratitude** for your continued **patronage**! Signed,
The Bella **Salon Staff**

Get ready!

1 **Before you read the passage, talk about these questions.**

1 At what time do the hair and beauty salons open and close in your area?

2 What are the off days for those types of businesses in your town?

Reading

2 **Read the announcement from Bella's salon. Then, mark the following statements as true (T) or false (F).**

1 __ The new business hours will take effect from early fall.

2 __ The extended business hours will begin at the beginning of June.

3 __ Fridays and Saturdays are currently off days at the salon.

Vocabulary

3 **Read the sentence and choose the correct word.**

1 The hairdressers are closed on **holidays / weekdays** because those days are for celebrating special occasions.

2 Sundays are **business hours / off days** at the salon, so the salon's staff will not be working on those days.

3 The salon treats its **extended / esteemed** clientele with courtesy and respect.

4 **Check (✓) the sentence that uses the underlined part correctly.**

1 __ A A salon's <u>regular hours</u> are the hours during the day when it is usually closed.

__ B The salon's owner thanked the loyal client for his <u>patronage</u>.

2 __ A The new policy is not <u>in effect</u> yet, so we continue to follow the old rules.

__ B The employees are not required to come to work during <u>business hours</u>.

3 __ A The salon's <u>hours of operation</u> are from 8:00 am to 10:00 pm every day.

__ B The regular <u>clients</u> complain that the staff always <u>meets the needs</u> of its visitors to the salon.

5 🎧 **Listen and read the announcement from Bella's salon again. When will the regular business hours change?**

Listening

6 🎧 **Listen to a conversation between a receptionist and a caller. Choose the correct answers.**

1 What is the dialogue mostly about?

- **A** which days are off days at the salon
- **B** the best time to schedule an appointment
- **C** where to find a salon that is open on Sundays
- **D** the hours of operation during the summer

2 What will the caller most likely do next?

- **A** contact another salon
- **B** schedule an appointment
- **C** change her work schedule
- **D** complain about the hours

7 🎧 **Listen again and complete the conversation.**

Receptionist:	Thank you for calling the Bella Salon. How can I help you?
Caller:	Hi. Until what time will you be **1** _____ _____ today?
Receptionist:	Today, we'll be accepting appointments **2** _____ _____ .
Caller:	Hmm … Well, I don't **3** _____ _____ _____ until six. I guess that would be too late huh?
Receptionist:	I'm afraid so, ma'am. But you can schedule an appointment for next Monday. Our summer business hours will **4** _____ _____ _____ then.
Caller:	Oh really? What are the **5** _____ _____ ?
Receptionist:	Starting Monday, we'll be open from 9:00 am to 8:00 pm every weekday.
Caller:	And the weekends?
Receptionist:	We'll be open from 8:00 am to 5:00 pm on Saturday.
Caller:	So, I can schedule an appointment for next Monday at 6:30?
Receptionist:	Of course. Just give me your name and **6** _____ _____ .

Speaking

8 **With a partner, act out the roles below based on Task 7. Then, switch roles.**

> **USE LANGUAGE SUCH AS:**
>
> *Until what time will you be taking appointments?*
> *We'll be accepting appointments until …*
> *What are the summer hours?*

Student A: You are a caller. Ask Student B questions to find out:

- until what time the salon will be taking appointments
- what the extended business hours are

Student B: You are a receptionist at Bella Salon. Answer Student A's questions.

Writing

9 **You are a salon owner. Use the announcement and the conversation from Task 8 to write an announcement to clients advertising the salon's new business hours. Make sure to mention:**

- When the new hours begin
- Which days are off days
- What the new hours of operation are

Bella **Salon**

New Business Hours

_____
_____
_____
_____
_____
_____
_____

appointment book

schedule

receptionist

Stylist

Get ready!

❶ Before you read the passage, talk about these questions.

1   Why do people make appointments at a salon?

2   What information do you need to give, to make an appointment?

Reading

❷ Read the note from a beauty salon. Then, choose the correct answers.

1   What is the note about?

   A   this weekend's openings

   B   who requires appointments

   C   how to schedule an appointment

   D   the best time to pencil in a client

2   What is true about weekends?

   A   There are more walk-in appointments than during the week.

   B   Most of the stylists only work then.

   C   Business hours are extended then.

   D   There are few spaces available then.

3   What can you infer from the note?

   A   Jen has worked at Bella the longest.

   B   There are two different appointment books.

   C   Clients don't always get their desired slot.

   D   Rates are higher on the weekends.

Thursday, June 6

Time	Stylist		
	Olivia Carpenter	Alyssa Mann	Alex Smith
9:00 am	Beth Adams Perm		
10:00 am			Audrey Young Bridal Make-up
11:00 am		Tim Harper Haircut	
12:00 am			

Hi Jen,

Welcome to the Bella Salon family. We are happy to have you as part of our team. On your first day, you will learn how to **schedule** appointments. Please follow these steps every time you **confirm** an appointment.

First, when you take a call ask the client in a friendly voice, what day and time he or she wants to **book** an appointment for. Remember, most of our **openings** are during the **workweek**. **Weekend** spaces are very limited.

Next, ask the client which stylist he or she wants to see. Always **consult** the **appointment book** to see which stylists are available.

What if a **stylist** is completely booked? Ask the client if it would be possible to make the appointment for another date or time. Tell the client what other **time slots** are available, and then **pencil in** the client for one of these openings.

Finally, **confirm** the appointment with the client.

Let me know if you have any questions.

Olivia

Vocabulary

❸ Match the words (1-8) with the definitions (A-H).

1   __ confirm   5   __ time slot

2   __ pencil in   6   __ limited

3   __ appointment book   7   __ consult

4   __ weekend   8   __ workweek

   A   an item that is used to record time slots

   B   a time set aside for appointments

   C   the last two days of the week

   D   the hours or days worked during a week

   E   to make certain

   F   available in short supply

   G   to get information or advice

   H   to schedule an appointment

4 Place a (✓) next to the response that answers the question.

1   Are there any openings for Tuesday?

   A __ No, there are none available.

   B __ Our business hours have changed.

2   Did you schedule an appointment today?

   A __ I arranged one for 3:00 pm.

   B __ The salon is open until 8:00 pm.

3   Did Miss Li call to book an appointment?

   A __ She used to work as a stylist.

   B __ Yes, she scheduled one for 10 am.

4   Do you know how to take appointments?

   A __ Yes, I used to schedule them at my old job.

   B __ I checked the available time slots.

5 🎧 Listen and read the note from Bella's salon again. When is it difficult to make an appointment at the salon?

Listening

6 🎧 Listen to a conversation between a receptionist and a caller. Mark the following statements as true (T) or false (F).

1   __ There are no open slots on Friday.

2   __ The caller requests a specific stylist.

3   __ The woman confirms the appointment.

7 🎧 Listen again and complete the conversation.

Receptionist: Hi, **1** _____ _____ the Bella Salon.

Caller: Hello. I'd like to **2** _____ _____ _____ for a haircut.

Receptionist: Okay. When would you like to **3** _____ the appointment for?

Caller: Um, **4** _____ _____ this Friday at two?

Receptionist: Let me check the **5** _____ book. Uh oh. I'm afraid all our stylists are booked at that time. But I do have an **6** _____ at 3:15. Does that work?

Caller: Sounds good to me.

Receptionist: All right. Do you have a stylist request?

Caller: No, anyone's fine.

Receptionist: Okay then. I'll **7** _____ _____ _____ with Alex. Now, I just need your name and telephone number.

Caller: My name is Joshua McCloud. And my number is 321-9021

Receptionist: Okay, Mr. McCloud. We'll see you at 3:15 this Friday!

Speaking

8 With a partner, act out the roles below based on Task 7. Then, switch roles.

USE LANGUAGE SUCH AS:

I'd like to make an appointment for ...

Sounds good to me.

I'll set you up with ...

Student A: You are a receptionist at Bella Salon. Talk to Student B about:

● what date he or she wants to schedule an appointment for

● what openings are available

● if he or she has a stylist request

Student B: You are a caller who is trying to make an appointment. Respond to Student A's questions.

Make up a name and telephone number for your appointment.

Writing

9 You are a salon owner. Use the note and the conversation from Task 8 to write scheduling advice for receptionists. Make sure to mention:

● What steps are involved

● How one finds out which stylists are available

● What happens if a stylist is booked

Bella
Salon Notes:

_____
_____
_____
_____

5 Shampoo

shampoo chair

lather

hose / nozzle

nape

Get ready!

① **Before you read the passage, talk about these questions.**

1 How is getting a shampoo at a salon different from washing your hair at home?

2 What are some things a stylist should consider when shampooing a client's hair?

Reading

② **Read the excerpt from a text book for hairdressers. Then, mark the following statements as true (T) or false (F).**

1 __ Keeping a finger over the nozzle helps the stylist determine the water temperature.

2 __ The textbook suggests using a cape to protect the client's face and neck from getting wet.

3 __ Stylists should use a higher water pressure when rinsing the shampoo.

Vocabulary

③ **Write a word that is similar in meaning to the underlined part.**

1 Fiona sat in the <u>seat that is specially designed for giving professional shampoos</u> and waited for the stylist to wet her hair.
_ h _ m _ _ _   _ h a _ _

2 Mark used a <u>roughly the same amount and size as a quarter coin</u> amount of hair gel.
q _ a _ _ e _-s _ _ e _

3 Vernon put soap on the hand towel and worked it into a <u>mass of small white bubbles</u>.
l _ t _ _ _

4 The stylist made sure she kept her finger over the <u>long tube that carries water</u>.   _ o _ e

Shampooing Made Easy

Preparation
- Advise the client to remove all jewelry.
- Instruct the client to sit in the **shampoo chair**.
- **Wrap** a towel around the client's shoulders, **tucking in** the ends to secure it.
- **Drape** a plastic cape over the towel.

Lather
- Test the water temperature and pressure. Make sure the water is **lukewarm**. Keep your finger over the **nozzle** each time you use the **hose**. That way, you can monitor the water temperature.
- Use the hose to **saturate** the client's hair and scalp with water. **Cup** your hand over the client's hairline and **nape** to protect them from getting wet.
- Rub a **quarter-sized** amount of **shampoo** between your hands.
- Then, use your fingertips to apply the shampoo to the client's hair, gently working it into a **lather**.

Rinsing
- Protect the client's face with one hand.
- Then, increase the water pressure on the hose and rinse the shampoo from the hair.
- Finally, **towel dry** the client's hair.

Beauty Salon Journal

④ **Fill in the blanks with the correct word or phrase:** *nape, saturated, towel dries, nozzle, wrap, draped, cups, tucked, lukewarm.*

1 Rick turned on the faucet and the water came out of the _____ .

2 Jessica doesn't like using blow dryers, so she always _____ her hair.

3 The warm water ran down the client's _____ .

4 Greg doesn't like the water to be either too hot or too cold and always uses _____ water.

5 Janie always _____ her hands over her eyes to stop soap from getting in.

6 You must _____ a towel around the client's shoulders before you start.

7 Vivian _____ the cape under her son's chin, before she started to shampoo.

8 Quentin _____ the woman's long hair with water.

9 Beth _____ a cape over her client's shoulders.

5 🎧 **Listen and read the excerpt from a textbook again. Why should a stylist keep their finger over the nozzle of the hose while wetting the client's hair?**

Listening

6 🎧 **Listen to a conversation between a stylist and a client getting her hair washed. Choose the correct answers.**

1 What is the conversation mostly about?

 A protecting valuables during a shampoo

 B the best water temperature to use during a shampoo

 C the types of shampoos used in salons

 D making sure a client is comfortable during a shampoo

2 What is true about the woman?

 A She recently had a haircut.

 B She prefers hot water.

 C She wears glasses.

 D She does not have any jewelry.

7 🎧 **Listen again and complete the conversation.**

Stylist:	Good afternoon, Miss Jackson. What can I do for you today?
Client:	I'm just here for a shampoo.
Stylist:	Okay. Before we start, why don't you **1** _____ _____ your earrings and glasses? I wouldn't want them to get wet or damaged.
Client:	**2** _____ _____ .
Stylist:	Thank you. Now, I need you to take a seat and **3** _____ _____ in the chair for me. Are you comfortable?
Client:	Yes, **4** _____ _____ .
Stylist:	Now, let me know if the **5** _____ is okay.
Client:	Oh! That's a little **6** _____ _____ .
Stylist:	I'm sorry about that. How about now?
Client:	That's perfect.

Speaking

8 **With a partner, act out the roles below based on Task 7. Then, switch roles.**

USE LANGUAGE SUCH AS:

Before we start, why don't you …

Now, I need you to …

Let me know if the temperature is okay.

Student A: You are a stylist at Bella Salon. Talk to Student B about:

● preparing for the shampoo

● his or her comfort during the shampoo

Student B: You are a client who is going to receive a shampoo. Follow the instructions from Student A and respond to his or her questions.

Writing

9 **You are a hair stylist. Use the except and the conversation from Task 8 to write instructions for a new employee on giving a shampoo. Write about:**

● What to do before the shampoo

● How to determine the client's comfort level

Bella
Salon   Notes:

perm

applicator bottle

APPLICATOR

protective gloves

hood-type dryer

curlers

perm rods

tail comb

RINGLET PERM SYSTEMS
An Hermosa Beauty Salon Professional Product

Ringlet Perm Systems will give your clients the curls they crave. We offer **alkaline**, **acid*** and **exothermic perm** kits, so you can choose the formula that best suits your client's hair type. Ringlet Perm Kits include everything you need to give a professional perm, including:

Protective gloves, **caps**** and **applicator bottles**
A **tail comb** to block hair into sections
Formers in a variety of shapes and sizes***
A gentle **neutralizer** that helps hair hold the curl for up to three months
An **after-perm aid** that conditions and replenishes hair

Only available in salons!

*   Acid kits require a **hood-type dryer**
**   Remember, all perm kits contain **caustic** chemicals. Be sure to use equipment to protect yourself and your clients.
*** Professionals can also use their own **rods** and **curlers** with the Ringlet Perm Systems

Get ready!

1 Before you read the passage, talk about these questions.

1   What are some ways to make hair curly?
2   What are some of the things needed in a salon to give clients a perm?

Reading

2 Read the advertisement for a new product. Then, mark the following statements as true (T) or false (F).

1   __ Each of the perm kits require a specific type of hair dryer to work.
2   __ Ringlet perm kits are only available to professional stylists.
3   __ Protective equipment is included with the perm kits.

Vocabulary

3 Check (✓) the sentence that uses the underlined part correctly.

1   __ A   Lori squeezed the dye from the applicator bottle.
    __ B   Ellen placed the liquid in a neutralizer while she prepared her hair.

2   __ A   Kerry sat under a hood-type dryer until her hair wasn't wet anymore.
    __ B   Jerry used the after-perm aid to make his hair straight again.

3   __ A   Jean put a cap around her shoulders.
    __ B   Will wrapped the hair around the rods in order to create curls.

4 Match the words (1-7) with the definitions (A-E).

1   __ acid perm   5   __ neutralizer
2   __ exothermic perm   6   __ caustic
3   __ alkaline perm   7   __ curlers
4   __ former

A   small plastic cylinders used to create curly hair
B   a type of perm that contains chemicals that create heat, so no external heat is needed
C   a type of perm that uses acid to create curls in the hair
D   a type of perm that uses alkaline to create curls in the hair
E   a piece of wire covered in foam used to curl hair
F   a substance that stops the chemicals that create a perm
G   able to destroy or seriously damage something it comes into contact with

5 🎧 **Listen and read the advertisement for a new product again. How does an acid perm kit differ from an alkaline perm kit?**

Listening

6 🎧 **Listen to the conversation between a stylist and a client. Choose the correct answers.**

1 According to the conversation, one benefit of using an alkaline perm kit is that it _____ .

   A requires heat to work

   B produces long-lasting effects

   C prevents damaging dye jobs

   D is gentler than other types of perms

2 What is probably true about the woman?

   A She styles her hair with a blow dryer.

   B She has naturally curly hair.

   C She does not have dyed hair.

   D She has had an acid perm before

7 🎧 **Listen again and complete the conversation.**

Stylist:	Is this the first time you've had a perm?
Client:	Yes. I'm excited about having **1** _____ hair.
Stylist:	Great. So, today, I'll use an **2** _____ _____ for your perm.
Client:	Just out of curiosity, why don't you use an acid or exothermic **3** _____ ?
Stylist:	Acid perms are much gentler on hair, but they're typically for people with hair that's damaged or **4** _____ - _____ . Your hair is in perfect condition.
Client:	Oh, I see.
Stylist:	Also, acid and exothermic perms require heat to work.
Client:	But alkaline perms don't?
Stylist:	That's right. That's why they're called **5** '_____ _____ '.
Client:	Which of them produces the best results?
Stylist:	Well, alkaline perms **6** _____ _____ last the longest.
Client:	That's great. I want long-lasting curls!

Speaking

8 **With a partner, act out the roles below based on Task 7. Then, switch roles.**

USE LANGUAGE SUCH AS:

Is this the first time you've had a perm?

Today, I'll use a(n) … for your perm.

Which of them produces the best results?

> **Student A:** You are a stylist. Ask Student B questions to determine hair type. Then, choose the best perm solution. Explain:
> - why the formula you chose is the best
> - the advantages of the formula you chose

> **Student B:** You are a client. Respond to Student A's questions. Then, ask about:
> - why he or she chose the formula
> - the advantages of the formula

Writing

9 **You are a stylist that used the Ringlet Perm System. Use the conversation from Task 8 to write a letter to the company describing your positive experience with a perm kit. Make sure to mention:**

- Which type of perm you used
- Why you decided to use that type of perm
- The results of the perm

Dear Sir or Madam, _____

_____

_____

_____

_____

_____

_____

_____

Yours faithfully,

7 Straightening

flat iron

smooth

Hair Straightening at Bella Salon

Tired of blow drying your hair straight every morning with your own **hair straightening kit**? Visit the stylists at Bella Salon for longer lasting straightening solutions.

Chemical Relaxers

Our stylists use a **no-lye solution** that creates soft, silky hair in just minutes. Results typically last 4-6 weeks. Our most affordable straightening option.

Keratin Treatment

This treatment is ideal for clients seeking semi-permanent results. A stylist applies a special solution into the hair, then **flat irons** the hair straight to **activate** the chemicals.* This treatment creates **glossy, frizz-free** hair for 2-4 months.

Thermal Reconditioning

Thermal reconditioning is a multi-step **procedure** that produces permanent results (unlike other straightening methods). That means you only have to treat **new hair growth**! First, the stylist applies a chemical solution. Next, the stylist adds a **serum** to the hair and flat irons it several times to make the hair **smooth**. This procedure is lengthy, but the results are worth it!

*Please note that clients are advised not to wash their hair for four days following keratin treatment to **ensure** the best results

Get ready!

① Before you read the passage, talk about these questions.

1 Why do some people straighten their hair?

2 What are some ways that people straighten their hair?

Reading

② Read this excerpt from a hair salon's website. Then, choose the correct answers.

1 What is the main topic of the web page?

   A ways hair straighteners can last longer

   B costs of straightening methods

   C various straightening options at a salon

   D how to straighten hair using home kits

2 What is true about keratin treatment?

   A It is activated by water.

   B It is the most costly treatment.

   C Heat reduces its effectiveness.

   D Immediate washing is not advisable.

3 How is thermal reconditioning different from the other straightening methods?

   A It requires heat styling to be effective.

   B It straightens hair permanently.

   C It can be done at home.

   D It is completed within minutes.

Vocabulary

③ Check (✓) the sentence that uses the underlined part correctly.

1 __ A Allison uses a <u>serum</u> to dry her hair.

   __ B The <u>no-lye solution</u> is gentle.

2 __ A My hair feels soft and <u>smooth</u>.

   __ B Jane's hair was <u>oily</u> and dry.

3 __ A Meg noticed some <u>new hair growth</u> around her hairline.

   __ B I <u>activated</u> the hairdryer by unplugging it.

④ Match the words (1-6) with the definitions (A-F).

1 __ serum   4 __ procedure

2 __ ensure   5 __ thermal reconditioning

3 __ frizz-free   6 __ keratin treatment

A a permanent hair straightening method that involves applying a chemical solution and activating the chemicals by heat

B not having unmanageable tight curls

C to make certain of something

D the steps or actions to do something

E a semi-permanent straightening method that involves applying a solution on the hair and activating the chemicals by heat

F a liquid with a high amount of substances that perform a specific function

5 🎧 Listen and read the excerpt from a hair salon's website again. What are two reasons why flat irons are used for straightening hair?

Listening

6 🎧 Listen to a conversation between a receptionist and a client. Mark the following statements as true (T) or false (F).

1 __ The client wants temporary straightening.

2 __ The treatment requires a flat iron.

3 __ The client chooses the keratin treatment.

7 🎧 Listen again and complete the conversation.

Receptionist:	Welcome to Bella Salon. How can I help you?
Client:	Good morning. I'd like to get **1** _____ _____ _____ .
Receptionist:	Well, we offer various methods. I'm sure we have one that will work for you.
Client:	Great!
Receptionist:	Are you looking for temporary or **2** _____ results?
Client:	Um, I want something **3** _____ - _____ .
Receptionist:	I know just the thing. We have a keratin treatment that lasts for about four months.
Client:	That sounds perfect. Does that involve any **4** _____ _____ ?
Receptionist:	Yes, it does. The hair is flat ironed. The heat is necessary to **5** _____ _____ _____ .
Client:	Is there anything else I should know about the treatment?
Receptionist:	Well, you won't be able to wash your hair for four days afterwards.
Client:	Wow! If that's the case, I'd rather try a different method.

serum

glossy

hair straightening kit

Speaking

8 With a partner, act out roles below based on Task 7. Then, switch roles.

Student A: You are a receptionist at Bella Salon. Talk to Student B about:

● how long the client wants the results to last

● what straightening options are available

Student B: You are a client who wants your hair straightened. Ask student A questions about:

● the process for the suggested treatments

● additional information about the method

Writing

9 Imagine that you are a stylist. Use the excerpt and the conversation from Task 8 to write a short paragraph about straightening hair. Make sure to mention the following:

● Which straightening method you prefer

● Why you prefer it and what the benefits are

17

8 Hair coloring

chestnut

dark brown

light brown

purple-black

auburn

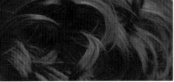
copper

honey blonde

platinum

Get ready!

① **Before you read the passage, talk about these questions.**

1 Why do some people color their hair?

2 What are some advantages of different hair colors?

Reading

② **Read the information from a magazine article. Then, mark the following true (T) or false (F).**

1 __ Chestnut hair is easy to maintain.

2 __ Healthy red hair holds color well.

3 __ Blonde shades have low maintenance.

Vocabulary

③ **Place the words and phrases from the word bank under the correct heading.**

auburn   **platinum**   chestnut
light brown   **copper**   **honey blonde**
golden blonde   dark brown

Brunette	Redhead	Blonde

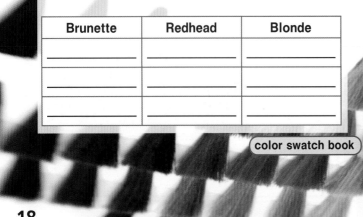
color swatch book

Hairdresser Today - April Edition

The Best Color for You!
Choose from our new **color swatch book**

Browns and Blacks

Choose from our new **color swatch book**. There are plenty of reasons to go **brunette**. Maintenance is very easy, and dark hair reflects a lot of light, so it looks very shiny. But remember, if you're thinking about a very dark color (like **blue-black**) consult a professional. Once you dye your hair black, it is very difficult to change it back.

Hot colors
chestnut, dark brown, light brown

Reds

Do you enjoy getting a lot of attention? Then, try a head-turning shade of red. **Redheads** must have very healthy hair in order for the hair color to last for a long time. But it's worth it! Just stay away from **purple-black** tones, which appear unnatural.

Hot colors
auburn, copper

Blondes

For a youthful, energetic look, try **blonde** shades. But it may take time to find the right shade to match your skin tone. Also, blonde hair costs a lot of money and time to maintain.

Hot colors
honey blond, platinum, golden blond

④ **Write a word that is similar in meaning to the underlined part.**

1 Tara has decided to dye her hair a pale yellow color.   _ l _ n _ _

2 The stylist advised Sara against getting <u>very dark black with tones of blue</u> hair because it doesn't match her skin tone.
   _ _ u _-_ l _ c k

3 Helen is the only <u>person with brown hair</u> in her class.   _ r _ n _ t _ _

5 🎧 **Listen and read the information from a magazine article again. What must someone consider if they want to dye their hair blonde?**

Listening

6 🎧 **Listen to a conversation between a stylist and client at a hair salon. Choose the correct answers.**

1 What does the man help the woman with?
   A choosing a new hair color
   B maintaining a previous hair color
   C advising about hair care
   D picking the right hair cut

2 What is true about the woman?
   A She has never dyed her hair before.
   B She visits the salon every two weeks.
   C She has naturally dark hair.
   D She wants to look younger.

7 🎧 **Listen again and complete the conversation.**

Stylist: Good morning, Mrs McAllen. You're here for a **1** _____ _____ consultation, aren't you?

Client: That's right. I really want to change my look.

Stylist: Well, let's talk about your options. First, do you want to go lighter or **2** _____?

Client: I've always wanted to try **3** _____ hair.

Stylist: Okay, blonde is very popular. But you should know that you'd have to come in every 2 to 4 weeks for touch-ups.

Client: Wow, that could get **4** _____ .

Stylist: On the other hand, blonde hair typically makes women look younger.

Client: Really? Maybe blonde isn't such a great idea then. What are some low-maintenance options?

Stylist: Well, you have **5** _____ _____ hair. We could give you light brown instead.

Client: I want a bigger change from my natural color. How about red shades?

Stylist: I think copper red would look fantastic on you. And it's a lot easier to maintain than blonde.

Client: That sounds perfect! Let's see how I look as a **6** _____!

Speaking

8 **With a partner, act out the roles below based on Task 7. Then, switch roles.**

USE LANGUAGE SUCH AS:

I really want to change my look.

First, do you want to go lighter or darker?

I think … would look fantastic on you.

Student A: You are a stylist at Bella Salon. Talk to Student B about:
- his or her color preferences
- the color's advantages and disadvantages
- suitable colors for the client

Student B: You are a client. Based on Student A's advice, choose a hair color.

Writing

9 **You are a colorist. Use the conversation from Task 8 to write notes about the client's change of hair color. Write about:**
- The options
- The advantages of different hair colors

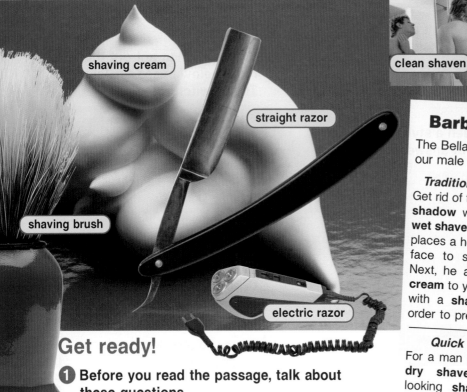

9 Barber service

shaving cream

straight razor

shaving brush

electric razor

clean shaven

five o'clock shadow

mustache

beard

Barber Services at Bella Salon

The Bella Salon offers the following services just for our male **clientele**.

Traditional Wet Shave Get rid of that **five o'clock shadow** with a traditional **wet shave**. First, our **barber** places a hot towel on your face to soften the skin. Next, he applies **shaving cream** to your face usually with a **shaving brush** in order to prevent **irritation**. Then, the barber uses a sharp **straight razor** to remove all unwanted hair from the face and neck. Once this is done, a **styptic pencil** is used to tend to **nicks** and **cuts**. Finally, **aftershave** is applied to soothe the skin and give the client a **clean shaven** feel.

Quick Dry Shave For a man on the run, the **dry shave** keeps you looking **sharp**. Using an **electric razor**, our barber works quickly to remove unwanted hair. Aftershave is available upon request.

Barber Service Add-ons:
Mustache Trim   Mustache and **Beard** Trim

Get ready!

❶ **Before you read the passage, talk about these questions.**

1 What are some grooming services for men?

2 What items do men use when they shave?

Reading

❷ **Read the poster from a salon. Then, choose the correct answers.**

1 What is true about the barber services at the Bella Salon?

   A They are available to men and women.

   B They include massage treatments.

   C They focus on maintenance of facial hair.

   D They are only offered during the evening.

2 According to the poster, which of the following is a difference between a wet shave and a dry shave?

   A the type of razor used

   B the price of the service

   C the kind of aftershave used

   D how sharp the razor is

3 What is probably true about men who choose dry shaves?

   A They have mustaches.

   B They do not get nicks or cuts.

   C They prefer not to use aftershave.

   D They are in a hurry.

Vocabulary

❸ **Choose the word that is closest in meaning to the underlined part.**

1 David needs to visit a barber to trim his <u>hair that covers the upper lip</u>.

   A mustache   **B** beard

   C five o'clock shadow

2 Alex entered the salon and asked for a(n) <u>type of shave that uses shaving cream and a razor</u>.

   A barber   **B** wet shave   **C** dry shave

3 The barber applied <u>a liquid that is put on a man's face after shaving</u> to the client's face.

   A aftershave   **B** razor burn

   C shaving cream

4 The salon does good business because it has a very loyal <u>collection of clients</u>.

   A electric razor   **B** barber   **C** clientele

5 Michael applied an ointment to his face to treat the <u>small cut</u> he received from his razor.

   A five o'clock shadow   **B** nick

   C aftershave

4 Read the sentences and choose the correct meaning of the underlined word(s).

1 John cannot use the <u>electric razor</u> because there's no electricity for an hour.

   A a rotating blade that runs on electricity

   B a long blade that folds out from the handle

   C cream that is put on a person's face before shaving

2 The bank requires all of its male employees to be <u>clean-shaven</u>.

   A without hair on the face

   B have hair that covers the upper lip

   C have the lower half of the face covered in hair

3 James always uses <u>shaving cream</u> because he wants to prevent irritation.

   A liquid applied after shaving to smell nice

   B a type of cream which removes hair

   C a cream used during a wet shave

5 🎧 Listen and read the poster from a salon again. What is a styptic pencil used for?

Listening

6 🎧 Listen to a conversation between a stylist and a client. Mark the following statements as true (T) or false (F).

1 __ The wet shave takes longer than the dry shave.

2 __ Most clients prefer the dry shave.

3 __ The client wants to have his mustache trimmed.

7 🎧 Listen again and complete the conversation.

Barber: Hello, Mr. Ridley. What can I do for you today?

Client: I'd like a **1** _____ , please.

Barber: Okay. We have a few shaving services.

Client: Can you tell me about them?

Barber: Sure. Most clients go with a traditional **2** _____ _____ .

Client: What does that involve?

Barber: First, I'll cover your skin with **3** _____ _____ . Then, I'll use a **4** _____ _____ to get rid of the hair.

Client: How long does that take?

Barber: It takes about 45 minutes.

Client: Do you have a faster shaving service?

Barber: Yes, we also offer a 20 minute **5** _____ _____ . I would use an electric razor for that.

Client: Electric razors always give me **6** _____ _____ , so I'll have a wet shave, please.

Speaking

8 With a partner, act out the roles below based on Task 7. Then, switch roles.

USE LANGUAGE SUCH AS:

I'd like a shave, please.

Can you tell me about them?

I'll have ..., please.

Student A: You are a barber at the Bella Salon. Talk to Student B about:

● the reason for his visit

● what choice of service the salon offers

● the processes and tools involved

Student B: You are a client at the Bella Salon. Ask Student A questions about the services offered. Then, tell Student A what service you want.

Writing

9 You are a barber. Use the poster and the conversation from Task 8 to write a notice about your barber services. Write about:

● available services

● how long various shaves take

● types of razors used for various shaves.

Services available: _____

_____

Time: _____

_____

Types of razors: _____

_____

21

hair loss

split ends

Get ready!

1 **Before you read the passage, talk about these questions.**

1 What can damage hair?

2 What are some ways that professionals treat damaged hair?

Reading

2 **Read the pamphlet from a salon. Then, choose the correct answers.**

1 What is the main idea of the pamphlet?

   A common causes of split ends

   B steps to safely styling hair

   C advice for repairing hair problems

   D ways to avoid hair loss

2 According to the passage, what is true about hair loss?

   A It often occurs as people get older.

   B It usually happens to people with fine hair.

   C It makes the scalp feel itchy and dry.

   D It can be prevented by using certain styling products.

3 According to the passage, which is NOT a cause of split ends?

   A having hair permed often

   B styling hair through heat processes

   C trimming off hair ends

   D brushing hair carelessly

Caring for Damaged Hair
The Bella Salon's Solutions to Common Hair Problems

Dry scalp and dandruff

Washing and drying hair too often strips away the hair's natural oils, leading to dry, **itchy** and **flaky scalp**. We offer **herbal extract treatments** to help replenish natural oils to the scalp and slow down the process of **hair loss**.

Hair Loss

Thinning hair and **balding** are sometimes caused by aging, but is made worse by the overuse of styling products. Try Bella's **volume-boosting** hair products to make your hair look thicker. These products also work wonders for clients with **fine hair**.

Split Ends

Over-processed hair is often visibly damaged. Regular perms and coloring, heat styling, and rough brushing can cause hair to split. We suggest starting with a trim to snip off **split ends**, then treating the hair with a **leave-in conditioner** for strong, healthy hair.

Feel free to ask our expert stylists for other tips and products on offer to care for your hair.

Vocabulary

3 **Read the sentence pair. Choose where the words best fit the blanks.**

1 **dandruff / hair loss**

   Jim's hair is not thick anymore because of his _____ .

   Sara's scalp is dry and _____ falls from her head.

2 **herbal extract treatment / leave-in conditioner**

   Rusty didn't wash out the _____ so that it properly hydrated his hair.

   Lemon balm and lavender are the main ingredients in the _____ .

3 **over-processed / balding**

   Kay's hair is _____ because she used to dye and perm it a lot.

   Now that Sam is _____ , he doesn't have much hair to brush.

4 Fill in the blanks with the correct words and phrases:
itchy, flaky, thinning hair, fine hair, split ends.

1 Janie has _____ that falls out easily.

2 Jessica gets her hair trimmed regularly, in order to get rid of her _____ .

3 Jason could not help scratching his _____ scalp.

4 Tina's skin is _____ and it falls off in flat pieces.

5 Leslie's _____ does not hold styles well and needs more volume.

5 🎧 Listen and read the pamphlet from a salon again. Why would someone with fine hair use volume-boosting hair products?

Listening

6 🎧 Listen to a conversation between a stylist and a client. Choose the correct answers.

1 What hair problem does the man suffer from?

   A thinning hair   **C** balding

   B split ends   **D** dandruff

2 What will the client most likely do next?

   A use his old shampoo and conditioner

   B go to a different hair salon

   C buy a remedy for his hair problem

   D complain about an itchy scalp

7 🎧 Listen again and complete the conversation.

Stylist: Okay, Mr. Johnson, I'm all done with your **1** _____ . How does that look to you?

Client: It's great. Thanks very much.

Stylist: There's something I want to mention.

Client: Sure, what is it?

Stylist: While I was cutting your hair, I noticed that you have **2** _____ .

Client: Oh? But I shampoo and condition my hair regularly.

Stylist: That might actually be the problem.

Client: What do you mean?

Stylist: You see, Mr. Johnson, the chemicals in shampoos often causes a dry, **3** _____ scalp.

Client: I had no idea. What should I do?

Stylist: I know of a(n) **4** _____ _____ _____ that restores the scalp's natural oil. That might help.

Client: Sounds great. Is that **5** _____ here? I'll buy some now.

Stylist: Yes, sir. You can get it here.

Speaking

8 With a partner, act out the roles below based on Task 7. Then, switch roles.

USE LANGUAGE SUCH AS:

There's something that I wanted to mention.

While I was cutting your hair, I noticed that …

What should I do?

Student A: You are a stylist at Bella Salon. Talk to Student B about:

• a hair problem you noticed

• the causes for the hair problem

• a suggestion for fixing the problem.

Student B: You are a client at the Bella Salon. Tell Student A what you've done about the problem and ask for their advice.

Writing

9 You are a stylist at a salon. Use the pamphlet and the conversation in Task 8 to write instructions for treating a hair problem that your client has. Write about:

• what the symptoms of the problem are

• what causes the problem

• how the problem can be solved

Symptoms: _____

_____

_____

Causes: _____

_____

Solution: _____

Get ready!

1 **Before you read the passage, talk about these questions.**

1 Why is it important to have a professional manicure?

2 What are some items that professionals use during a manicure?

A PROFESSIONAL'S GUIDE TO MANICURES

Remove the Old Nail Polish
Put some **nail polish remover** on a **cotton ball** and press the cotton ball against the **nail plate**. To prevent damage, be sure to only use **non-acetone** remover on natural nails.

Shape the Nails
For a natural look, file the nail into an **oval** shape. **Square** tips, however, are very trendy. Another popular nail shape is **squoval**, which is a primarily square shape with rounded sides. The squoval shape is often used in **French manicures**.

Prepare for **Enamel**
Soak the nails and carefully remove overgrown **cuticles**. Use a buffer to eliminate **ridges** from the nail. You may follow this procedure with a **paraffin wax treatment** to moisturize the hands and cuticles.

Apply Nail Polish
Using 3-4 even strokes per nail, apply a thin layer of the **enamel**. Then, ask the client to place their hands inside the **nail dryer**.

French manicure

squoval

square

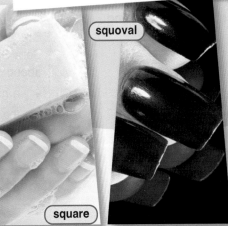

nail dryer

oval

Reading

2 **Read the excerpt from a cosmetology textbook. Then, choose the correct answers.**

1 What is the main topic of the excerpt?
  A popular nail shapes
  B different types of manicures
  C steps to giving a manicure
  D recommended nail products

2 According to the excerpt, what is the function of a paraffin wax treatment?
  A to remove overgrown cuticles
  B to relieve dry skin on hands
  C to prevent damage to the nail polish
  D to moisturize the ridges on the nail bed

3 What can be inferred about nail polish remover that contains acetone?
  A It is an older type of enamel remover.
  B It does not remove nail polish effectively.
  C It is harmful to natural nails.
  D It is typically found in salons.

Vocabulary

3 **Match the words (1-8) with the definitions (A-H).**

1 ___ cotton ball
2 ___ square
3 ___ oval
4 ___ non-acetone
5 ___ squoval
6 ___ nail polish remover
7 ___ paraffin wax treatment
8 ___ nail plate

A a shape with four corners
B a service that moisturizes dry skin with a soft and warm substance
C the hard part of the nail that can be painted
D a liquid that takes off nail color
E a round or curved shape
F a pad made from a soft, absorbent material
G a shape with four rounded corners
H not having a chemical that is commonly used to remove paint

4 Write a word that is similar in meaning to the underlined part.

1 Jane usually has a <u>nail treatment that involves painting the tip of the nails white</u> because it looks very elegant.
_ r e _ _ _   m _ _ _ _ _ _ _

2 The manicurist used a buffer to get rid of the <u>raised parts</u> on Jake's nails.   _ _ d g _ _

3 At the end of their manicure, clients put their hands in a <u>device that dries nail polish</u>.   _ a i _   d _ _ e _

4 Sara likes to apply a thin coat of <u>nail color</u> to her nails.
_ n _ m _ _

5 🎧 Listen and read the excerpt from a cosmetology textbook again. How do squoval and oval shaped nails differ?

Listening

6 🎧 Listen to a conversation between a nail technician and a client. Mark the following statements as true (T) or false (F).

1 _ The client goes by her first name.
2 _ The client wants a French manicure.
3 _ The nail technician chooses the nail color for the client.

7 🎧 Listen again and complete the conversation.

Nail Technician:	Hi, Miss Jensen. I'm Rick, and I'll be your nail technician today.
Client:	Hi Rick. You can call me Jan.
Nail Technician:	Very well, Jan. There are just a few things I want to ask you before we get started.
Client:	Okay.
Nail Technician:	First, do you have a specific kind of manicure in mind, like a **1** _____ _____?
Client:	No. I just want a regular manicure and **2** _____ _____.
Nail Technician:	In that case, please pick out your nail color before we start. You'll find our selection of **3** _____ _____ on the rack by the reception desk.
Client:	Did you have any other questions?
Nail Technician:	Oh, yes. Do you have a preference about the **4** _____ _____?
Client:	What are the choices?
Nail Technician:	We can do square, oval or **5** _____.
Client:	Um, squoval is good I guess.
Nail Technician:	Great! Go ahead and pick out your nail polish, then meet me at the **6** _____ _____ over there.

Speaking

8 With a partner, act out the roles below based on Task 7. Then, switch roles.

USE LANGUAGE SUCH AS:

Do you have a specific kind of manicure in mind?

Do you have a preference about the nail shape?

What are the choices?

Student A: You are a nail technician at Bella Salon. Talk to Student B about:

● the type of manicure / nail shape preference
● where to find the nail polishes
● where to meet for the manicure

Student B: You are a client and you want a manicure. Tell Student A what he/she should call you. Then, respond to Student A's questions.

Writing

9 You are a nail technician. Use the conversation from Task 8 to write a note about a client's manicure. Write about:

● how your client should be addressed
● what type of manicure the client wanted
● what nail shape the client chose

_____

_____

_____

_____

12 Manicure maintenance

maintain manicure

Get ready!

1 Before you read the passage, talk about these questions.

1 How can a manicure get damaged?

2 What are some ways to protect a manicure?

Reading

2 Read the magazine article. Then, choose the correct answers.

1 What is the main topic of the article?

A how to extend a manicure

B common problems with manicures

C how to apply topcoat properly

D how to save money on manicures

2 Why does the author suggest paying the nail technician before the manicure?

A to prevent being charged extra

B to get better service

C to avoid damaging the new manicure

D to be more relaxed

3 Which of the following is NOT a tip mentioned in the article?

A Allow each coat of paint to dry.

B Peel off old coats of nail polish first.

C Apply a topcoat over the paint every day.

D Take care of cuticles with hand cream.

Maintaining Your Manicure

By: Lindsay Jordan

Getting your nails done is always a treat, but do you know how to make your manicure last? Follow these simple tips to **maintain** beautiful nails:

Pay the **nail technician** before he or she starts. That way, you don't have to worry about digging around for the money later and accidentally **smudging** or **scratching** your new manicure. During the manicure, make sure the nail technician allows each **coat** of enamel to dry completely between **applications**. This prevents the paint from **shrinking** then **peeling** off later. Apply a clear **topcoat** to your nails daily in order to protect the enamel from **chipping** off. Be sure to apply the topcoat to the edges of the nails in order to create a protective **seal**.

Use a **hand cream** every day to keep your hands soft. This helps your manicure to stay looking great by preventing dry and **cracked** cuticles. Wear gloves while you do housework.

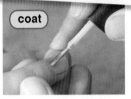
coat

chip

hand cream

Vocabulary

3 Use the words to fill in the blanks.

1 **scratched / smudged**

Lynn _____ her freshly-painted nails when she used her keyboard.

Rita _____ her polish as it wasn't dry.

2 **shrink / cracked**

The woman's _____ cuticles made her hands look ugly.

Some nail polishes do not _____ or peel off.

3 **seal / coat**

A topcoat acts as a protective _____ .

I always apply more than one _____ of polish.

4 Check (✓) the sentence that uses the underlined part correctly.

1 __ A Kara applies four clear <u>topcoats</u> of bright nail polish to get a deep color.

__ B Jane's manicure was ruined because most of the polish had <u>chipped</u> off.

2 __ A Wendy's cheap nail polish usually <u>peels</u> off after a day.

__ B Jo <u>maintains</u> her manicure well, so her nails are always broken.

3 __ A Gloria uses <u>hand cream</u> to prevent her hands from becoming too soft.

__ B The nail technician waited ten minutes after the first polish <u>application</u> to apply the second.

5 🎧 **Listen and read the magazine article again. Why is it important to apply a topcoat during a manicure?**

Listening

6 🎧 **Listen to a nail technician and a client. Mark the following statements as true (T) or false (F).**

1 ___ The nail technician tells the woman not to wash the dishes straight away.

2 ___ The beauty salon gives a complimentary pair of gloves with each manicure.

3 ___ The nail technician recommends reapplying topcoat every day.

7 🎧 **Listen again and complete the conversation.**

Nail Technician:	Okay, your manicure's all done. What do you think?
Client:	I love it! I just hope it lasts.
Nail Technician:	What do you mean?
Client:	Oh, nothing. It's just that the manicure always looks great for a couple of days. But then the polish starts **1**_____ _____ or gets scratched.
Nail Technician:	There are a couple of ways that you can avoid that, you know.
Client:	Really? Do you have any tips for making my manicure **2**_____ _____?
Nail Technician:	Sure. For one, be careful with your hands for the next few hours.
Client:	So I shouldn't wash dishes?
Nail Technician:	No, not right away, and when you do, be sure to wear gloves. That will help protect from smudging and **3**_____.
Client:	Okay, I can do that. What can I do to prevent **4**_____?
Nail Technician:	Try applying some **5**_____ over the polish every day.
Client:	What a great idea! Thanks for the **6**_____.

Speaking

8 **With a partner, act out the roles below based on Task 7. Then, switch roles.**

USE LANGUAGE SUCH AS:

I just hope it lasts.

Do you have any tips for making my manicure last longer?

Try …

Student A: You are a nail technician at the Bella Salon. Talk to Student B about:

● common manicure problems

● tips for making the manicure last longer

Student B: You are a client who just had a manicure. Tell Student A about what problems you usually have with your manicure.

Writing

9 **You are a nail technician. Use the conversation from Task 8 to write a note to your client about caring for her manicure. Write about:**

● common manicure problems

● ways to make manicures last longer

_____

_____

_____

_____

_____

_____

_____

_____

_____

_____

pluck

tweezers

irritated

waxing

Hair Today, Gone Tomorrow
Your Summer Guide to Hair Removal

Threading and Plucking

How it Works: A salon worker **twists** a thread and moves it across the skin, catching unwanted hairs between it. As the string untwists, it pulls out the hair. Any remaining hair is **plucked** out with **tweezers**.

Pros: Excellent for brow-shaping because it creates straight lines

Cons: Can lead to **ingrown hairs**

Waxing

How it Works: An **esthetician** applies hot wax to the skin and places a cloth or paper **strip** over the wax. Then, the worker quickly pulls off the strip, taking the hair along with it.

Pros: Lasts up to eight weeks because the hair is pulled out from the root

Cons: Painful and can leave skin red and **irritated**

Depilatory Creams

How it Works: The cream is applied directly to the skin and allowed to soak in, during which time the chemicals in the cream break down hair. Then, the hair can easily be washed off.

Pros: Painless and inexpensive

Cons: Can cause **chemical burns** and lasts for a few days

Get ready!

1 Before you read the passage, talk about these questions.

1 What parts of the body do people usually remove hair from?

2 What are some ways that people remove hair from their bodies?

Reading

2 Read the magazine article about hair removal. Then, mark the following statements as true (T) or false (F).

1 __ Threading achieves total hair removal.

2 __ Waxing involves pulling the hairs out from the root.

3 __ Depilatory creams last the longest of the hair removal methods mentioned.

Vocabulary

3 Read the sentence and choose the correct word.

1 Greg pulled out the hair with a pair of **tweezers / strips**.

2 The directions say to wash off the **depilatory cream / chemical burn** after ten minutes.

3 Jane prefers **waxing / threading** because it doesn't involve the use of hot substances or chemicals.

4 Damien **plucked / twisted** a stray hair from his eyebrow.

4 Match the words (1-7) with the definitions (A-G).

1 __ chemical burn   5 __ ingrown hair

2 __ irritated   6 __ esthetician

3 __ hair removal   7 __ pluck

4 __ strip

A a beauty salon worker

B to pull out

C damage to the skin because of exposure to chemicals

D a long and narrow piece

E the elimination of hair

F red and inflamed

G a hair that grows into the skin

⑤ 🎧 Listen and read the magazine article about hair removal again. Which hair removal method would be more suitable for someone with bushy eyebrows?

Listening

⑥ 🎧 Listen to a conversation between an esthetician and a client. Choose the correct answers.

1 Why does the woman visit the salon?

    A to ask for information about a new service

    B to have her eyebrows shaped

    C to get her legs waxed

    D to try a new hair removal method

2 What hair removal method does the woman choose?

    A waxing   **C** shaving

    B depilatory cream   **D** threading

⑦ 🎧 Listen again and complete the conversation.

Esthetician:	Good afternoon, Miss Jensen. So, you're just here to have your **1** _____ waxed, correct?
Client:	That's right.
Esthetician:	Waxing is great for removing hair from the legs. But you know, there are other methods that are better for **2** _____ - _____ .
Client:	Like what?
Esthetician:	Well, **3** _____ is our newest service.
Client:	I've never heard of it. Is it like shaving or using **4** _____ _____ ?
Esthetician:	Not quite. What I do is run a piece of twisted string along your skin. As the string untwists, it pulls the hair out.
Client:	And that gets all of the hair out?
Esthetician:	Most of it. Anything that the string misses, I pluck out with **5** _____ .
Client:	So what's so great about this technique?
Esthetician:	It creates **6** _____ _____ _____ , so it's perfect for brow-shaping. Would you like to try it out?
Client:	I don't see why not.

Speaking

⑧ With a partner, act out the roles below based on Task 7. Then, switch roles.

USE LANGUAGE SUCH AS:

There are other methods that are better for …

What I do is …

And that gets rid of the hair?

Student A: You are an esthetician at Bella Salon. Talk to Student B about:

- what hair removal service he or she is interested in
- a suggested hair removal method for Student B
- how the new method works

Student B: You are a client at the Bella Salon. Respond to Student A's questions then decide on a hair removal method based on the information Student A gives you.

Writing

⑨ You are an esthetician. Use the magazine article and the conversation from Task 8 to write a note to your client about a recommended hair removal method. Write about:

- how the method works
- what some advantages of the method are
- what some disadvantages of the method are

Get ready!

1 Before you read the passage, talk about these questions.

1 What are some common skin problems?

2 How do people care for skin?

blackhead

wrinkles

t-zone

sunscreen

Bella Beauty Salon
Skincare Questionnaire

Please fill out the questionnaire in order to get a **skincare regimen** designed just for you.

Name: _Jenny Willis_   Phone: _515-637-8089_   Age: _32_

Please place a check next to all the conditions that apply to you.

Blackheads	☑	Oily Skin	☑
Acne	☐	Sun spots	☐
Dry or flaky skin	☑	Capillaries	☑
Enlarged pores	☐	Wrinkles	☑

	Yes	No
Do you use **sunscreen**?	☐	☑
Do you smoke?	☐	☑
Have you had a bad reaction to products you applied to your skin?	☑	☐

If yes, please list the product and describe the reaction that you had.

Every time I use **sunscreen**, I develop a **rash**.

Describe your regular skincare routine:
I **cleanse** my face every morning and evening with a bar of soap. I apply moisturizer in the morning after washing, but not in the evening.

Describe your specific skin problems or concerns:
My skin is dry in some parts but I have a really oily **t-zone**.

Reading

2 Read the questionnaire about skincare. Then, choose the correct answers.

1 How does the salon use the questionnaire?

 A to learn how people use products

 B to create special routines

 C to design better sunscreen lotions

 D to find out the clients' skincare routines

2 Which is NOT true of the client's skin?

 A She has some facial oiliness.

 B She washes it twice a day.

 C She gets rashes.

 D She wears lotion to protect it from the sun.

3 What is true about Miss Willis?

 A She gave up smoking recently.

 B She has dry skin in the evening.

 C She uses moisturizer twice a day.

 D She gets rashes from skin products.

Vocabulary

3 Choose the word that is closest in meaning to the underlined part.

1 Isabel puts powder on her <u>forehead and nose area that tends to get oily</u>.

 A acne   **B** t-zone   **C** blackhead

2 James wears <u>a substance that protects skin from the sun's rays</u>.

 A sun spots   **B** wrinkles   **C** sunscreen

3 Kayla has a <u>group of red bumps</u> on her leg.

 A rash   **B** pore   **C** capillary

4 Check (✓) the sentence that uses the underlined part correctly.

1 __ **A** Wally's exercise <u>regimen</u> includes a daily jog.

 __ **B** Maxine buys shampoo and other <u>skincare</u> products.

2 __ **A** Josie has clear skin that is free of <u>acne</u>.

 __ **B** Abby developed enlarged <u>pores</u> because she smokes cigarettes.

3 __ **A** Harry sat in a <u>sun spot</u> and read a book.

 __ **B** Lloyd <u>cleanses</u> his face with a special soap.

5 🎧 **Listen and read the questionnaire about skincare again. Why doesn't Jenny Willis protect her skin when she's in the sun?**

Listening

6 🎧 **Listen to the conversation between a skincare consultant and a client. Choose the correct answers.**

1 What is the conversation mainly about?

   A why the woman doesn't use lotion

   B how to treat the woman's skin problems

   C why it is important to wear sunscreen

   D the causes of the woman's problems

2 What is the woman's main skin problem?

   A She has acne along her t-zone.

   B She often develops rashes.

   C She has both dry and oily skin.

   D She has many wrinkles on her face.

7 🎧 **Listen again and complete the conversation.**

Consultant:	Hello, Mrs Willis. I understand you have some concerns about your skin. Can you tell me more?
Client:	Sure. The biggest problem is that I have mostly **1** _____ _____ except for my t-zone. That part is always shiny!
Consultant:	I see, that's a very common problem.
Client:	Can I do anything to fix it?
Consultant:	I can recommend a **2** _____ specially formulated for your **3** _____ _____.
Client:	Marvelous!
Consultant:	There's something else I want to bring up. You said in your questionnaire that you don't use **4** _____.
Client:	No, it brings me out in a **5** _____.
Consultant:	I'm sorry to hear that, but you need to protect your skin from the sun.
Client:	I know, but I can't take the risk.
Consultant:	Sunscreen also prevents the formation of **6** _____ _____ and sun spots.
Client:	Well, I'd love you to find one that works for me.

Speaking

8 **With a partner, act out the roles below based on Task 7. Then, switch roles.**

USE LANGUAGE SUCH AS:

I understand you have some concerns …

The biggest problem is that …

Can I do anything to fix it?

Student A: You are a skincare consultant. Talk to Student B about:
- his or her biggest skincare problem
- your suggestions for fixing that problem
- a habit that may be harmful to Student B's skin

Student B: You are a client. Talk to Student A about:
- your biggest skincare problem
- a harmful habit that you have

Writing

9 **You are a skincare consultant. Use the questionnaire and the conversation from Task 8 to write about your client's skin problems. Write about:**
- your client's biggest skincare problem
- solution
- his or her bad skincare habit
- solution

Client's Problem: _____

_____

Solution: _____

_____

Client's Habit: _____

_____

Solution: _____

31

15 Spa facials

scrub

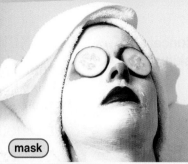
mask

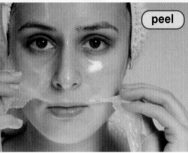
peel

pat

Bella Salon
Our Select Skincare Treatments

Your skin deserves the best, and at Bella Salon, we know exactly how to keep your skin looking fresh and beautiful. We offer several **facial treatments** for you to pick from.

Bella Express Facial
For clients with little time to spare, get a quick skin boost with the Bella Express Facial. We begin with a gentle **scrub** which is followed by a **mask**. We finish with a light **astringent** and moisturizer. This light facial is perfect for those with **sensitive skin**.
30 minutes $45

Bella Clear Complexion Facial
The Bella Clear Complexion Facial focuses on deep pore cleansing to help stop **breakouts** and give you the **complexion** you dream of. We start with a scrub that **exfoliates** by **sloughing** off dead skin. Then, we apply a **peel** that cleans pores before finishing with an oil-zapping **toner**.
60 minutes $90

Bella Signature Facial
Pamper yourself with the Bella Signature Facial. We begin by **steaming** your face to open up the pores. Next, we apply a mask that is specially blended for your skin type. After **patting** dry your skin, we finish with a relaxing head and shoulder massage.
60 minutes $120

Get ready!

❶ Before you read the passage, talk about these questions.

1 What are some services offered at spas?
2 Why do some people get facials at a spa?

Reading

❷ Read the poster about salon facial treatments. Then, choose the correct answers.

1 What is the main topic of the poster?
   A how to prevent break outs
   B different types of skin treatments
   C ways of treating different skin types
   D the process of a typical facial

2 How is the Bella Signature Facial different from the other facials offered at the salon?
   A It lasts longer than the other facials.
   B It includes treatments that are made especially for the client.
   C It involves the application of a facial mask.
   D Its price is determined by the products used during the facial.

3 What is the exfoliating scrub used for?
   A to take off dead skin
   B to pat skin dry
   C to relax the client
   D to open up the pores

Vocabulary

❸ Read the sentence pair. Choose where the words best fit the blanks.

1 **complexion / facial**
   Valerie went to the spa and had a _____ .
   Sally's _____ improved after she started a new skincare regime.

2 **scrub / astringent**
   Max used a _____ to get rid of the dead skin on his face.
   Ben uses a(n) _____ to help his skin feel firmer.

3 **mask / breakouts**
   Larry had fewer _____ when he started washing his face every night.
   Mindy let the _____ dry for ten minutes, then washed it off.

4 Match the words (1-6) with the definitions (A-F).

1 __ steam 3 __ peel 5 __ toner

2 __ exfoliate 4 __ slough 6 __ sensitive skin

A a substance used to tighten pores and make skin firm

B to rub a layer off

C a facial treatment that removes dead skin by pulling it off

D skin that reacts easily to products and conditions

E to expose something to hot water vapor

F to remove the top layer of skin in order to improve the appearance of the surface

5 🎧 Listen and read the poster about salon facial treatments again. Which treatment would someone choose if they had acne?

Listening

6 🎧 Listen to a conversation between an esthetician and a client. Mark the following statements as true (T) or false (F).

1 __ The client does not have a lot of time for the facial.

2 __ The man suggests the woman tries only the Clear Complexion Facial.

3 __ The woman wants a facial that helps her relax.

7 🎧 Listen again and complete the conversation.

Esthetician:	Good morning, ma'am. Have you decided on which facial you'd like today?
Client:	I'm still not sure. I was thinking about having the **1** _____ _____ .
Esthetician:	Are you short on time?
Client:	Not really. Why do you ask?
Esthetician:	Well, the Express facial takes only about half an hour.
Client:	Oh, that's not very long. What other options are there?
Esthetician:	You can try our Clear Complexion or Bella Signature Facials. Each one is about an hour long.
Client:	The Clear Complexion Facial, what does that involve?
Esthetician:	It includes a deep pore **2** _____ , a scrub and a **3** _____ . It helps clients achieve beautiful, clear **4** _____ .
Client:	That's nice, but I don't really need that. I really just want to **5** _____ .
Esthetician:	May I make a **6** _____ ?
Client:	By all means!
Esthetician:	If you want to relax, you might enjoy our Bella Signature Facial.

Speaking

8 With a partner, act out the roles below based on Task 7. Then, switch roles.

USE LANGUAGE SUCH AS:

Have you decided on which facial you'd like?

What other options are there?

What does that involve?

Student A: You are an esthetician at Bella Salon. Talk to Student B about:

● which facial he or she is interested in

● some drawbacks to his or her choice

● description of another type of facial

● suggestion for Student B's best facial

Student B: You are a client who wants a facial. Respond to Student A's questions.

Writing

9 You are an esthetician at a salon. Use the conversation in Task 8 to describe one of the facials at your salon. Write about:

● what is included in the facial

● how long it takes

acid perm [N-COUNT-U6] An **acid perm** is a type of chemical method to create curls in hair.

acne [N-UNCOUNT-U14] **Acne** is a skin problem characterized by painful red bumps on the skin.

activate [V-T-U7] To **activate** something is to make something work or happen.

after-perm aid [N-COUNT-U6] An **after-perm aid** is a product that conditions and replenishes hair after a perm.

aftershave [N-UNCOUNT-U9] **Aftershave** is a liquid that men usually put on their faces after shaving. The liquid contains substances that prevent infections.

alkaline perm [N-COUNT-U6] An **alkaline perm** is a type of chemical method to create curls in hair.

application [N-COUNT-U12] An **application** is the act of applying something, or putting something on.

applicator bottle [N-COUNT-U6] An **applicator bottle** is a container that is used to easily apply a substance on something.

apply [V-T-U11] To **apply** nail polish means to put it on.

appointment [N-COUNT-U1] An **appointment** is an arrangement to meet someone at a specific time and location.

arrive [V-I-U2] To **arrive** at a place is to reach it.

astringent [N-UNCOUNT-U15] An **astringent** is a liquid that causes skin to tighten and become firmer.

auburn [ADJ-U8] Hair that is **auburn** is a reddish brown color.

balding [ADJ-U10] If someone is **balding**, he or she is losing their hair.

barber [N-COUNT-U9] A **barber** is a person who cuts men's hair and provides shaving services.

beard [N-COUNT-U9] A **beard** is hair that covers the lower half of a man's face.

blackhead [N-COUNT-U14] A **blackhead** is a black spot on the skin.

blonde [N-COUNT-U8] **Blonde** describes a pale yellow, hair color.

blue-black [ADJ-U8] Hair that is **blue-black** is very dark black with blue tones in it.

boulevard [N-COUNT-U2] A **boulevard** is a wide street in a city with trees along each side.

breakout [N-COUNT-U15] A **breakout** is the occurrence of many skin problems at one time.

brunette [N-COUNT-U8] A **brunette** is a person with brown hair.

business hours [N PHRASE-U3] **Business hours** are the hours during the day when a business is open.

by appointment only [N PHRASE-U1] Something that is **by appointment only** is only available to someone who makes an appointment.

cap [N-COUNT-U6] A **cap** is a protective covering object that fits very closely to the head. It can be used when coloring hair.

capillary [N-COUNT-U14] A **capillary** is a thin blood vessel that lies under the skin. When it bursts, it becomes visible on the skin and appears red.

caustic [ADJ-U6] If something is **caustic**, it is able to destroy or seriously damage something it comes into contact with.

chemical burn [N-COUNT-U13] A **chemical burn** is damage to the skin because of exposure to chemicals.

chestnut [ADJ-U8] Hair that is **chestnut** is a dark reddish-brown color.

chip [V-I-U12] Something **chips** when it breaks off a larger piece.

cleanse [V-T-U14] To **cleanse** something is to clean it.

clean shaven [ADJ-U9] If a man is **clean shaven**, he has no hair on his face.

clientele [N-UNCOUNT-U9] **Clientele** is all of a business's clients.

coat [N-COUNT-U12] A **coat** is a thin layer of something that covers a surface.

color swatch book [N-COUNT-U8] A **color swatch book** is a presentation file consisting of samples of hair in the different colored dyes that a salon offers.

complexion [N-COUNT-U15] The **complexion** is the natural appearance of someone's skin, including color and texture.

copper [ADJ-U8] Hair that is **copper** is bright red.

cosmetology [N-UNCOUNT-U11] **Cosmetology** is the study or art of cosmetics and their use.

cotton ball [N-COUNT-U11] A **cotton ball** is a pad made from a soft, absorbent material.

cracked [ADJ-U12] Something is **cracked** when it is broken.

cup [V-T-U5] To **cup** your hands is to hold your hands in the shape of a cup.

cut [N-COUNT-U9] A **cut** is a small piercing done with a sharp instrument.

cuticle [N-COUNT-U11] A **cuticle** is the bit of skin around the nail.

curler [N-COUNT-U6] **Curlers** are plastic cylinders used to create a curl shape in hair.

dandruff [N-UNCOUNT-U10] **Dandruff** is a condition in which the scalp sheds small white pieces of dead skin.

dark brown [ADJ-U8] **Dark brown** hair is quite close to black in color.

depilatory cream [N-COUNT-U13] A **depilatory cream** is a thick liquid that contains chemicals which break down the hair and make it possible to wash the hair away.

destination [N-COUNT-U2] A **destination** is a place that someone is going to.

direct [V-T-U1] To **direct** someone is to show that person the way to a place.

directions [N-UNCOUNT-U2] **Directions** are instructions to describe how to get to a specific destination.

drape [V-T-U5] To **drape** something e.g. a material, is to place it over or across something else.

dry skin [ADJ-U14] **Dry skin** means skin lacking in natural oils.

dry shave [N-COUNT-U9] A **dry shave** is a type of shave that is done without shaving cream, usually with an electric razor.

electric razor [N-COUNT-U9] An **electric razor** is a razor with a rotating blade that is powered by electricity.

enamel [N-UNCOUNT-U11] **Enamel** is paint that turns shiny when it dries.

ensure [V-T-U7] To **ensure** something is to make certain of it.

esteemed [ADJ-U3] Someone who is **esteemed** is respected and held in high regard.

esthetician [N-COUNT-U13] An **esthetician** is someone connected with beauty and the study of it.

exfoliate [V-T-U15] To **exfoliate** your skin is to remove the top layer in order to improve the appearance of the surface.

exit [N-COUNT-U2] An **exit** is a road where traffic can leave a main road.

exothermic perm [N-COUNT-U6] An **exothermic perm** is a type of chemical way to curl hair where no external heat is needed.

extended [ADJ-U3] Something that is **extended** is made longer than normal.

facial [N-COUNT-U15] A **facial** is a treatment given to one's face that involves cosmetics that help the skin.

fine hair [N PHRASE-U10] **Fine hair** is hair that is thin and not very strong.

five o'clock shadow [N-UNCOUNT-U9] A **five o'clock shadow** is a darkness of the face that is caused by growing hair.

flaky [ADJ-U10] If something is **flaky**, pieces of it come off in small, flat pieces.

flat iron [N-COUNT-U7] A **flat iron** is a hairdressing tool that uses heat to straighten hair.

flat iron [V-T-U7] To **flat iron** hair means to straighten hair using a flat iron.

floor [N-COUNT-U2] A **floor** is a level in a building with many stories.

formers [N-COUNT-U6] **Formers** are flexible foam curlers used to make hair curly.

freeway [N-COUNT-U2] A **freeway** is a large road that is used for traveling fast across long distances.

French manicure [N-UNCOUNT-U11] A **French manicure** is a type of manicure. The nail tips are painted white and the rest of the nail is painted a color that matches the natural color of the nail, like light pink.

frizz-free [ADJ-U7] If something is **frizz-free**, it does not have unmanageable tight curls.

glossy [ADJ-U7] If something is **glossy**, it is shiny.

go straight [V PHRASE-U2] To **go straight** is to travel in a straight line.

golden blonde [ADJ-U8] Hair that is **golden blonde** is blonde with a golden tint.

gratitude [N-UNCOUNT-U3] **Gratitude** is the state of feeling grateful.

Glossary

greet [V-T-U1] To **greet** people is to welcome them when they arrive at a place.

guidelines [N-COUNT-U1] **Guidelines** are official advice about the appropriate way to act in a specific situation.

hair loss [N-UNCOUNT-U10] **Hair loss** is a condition in which someone loses hair volume.

hair straightening kit [N-COUNT-U7] A **hair straightening kit** is a set of tools or other items which can make a person's hair remain straightened for longer.

hair removal [N-UNCOUNT-U13] **Hair removal** is a process that eliminates unwanted hair.

hand cream [N-COUNT-U12] **Hand cream** is a thick liquid that moisturizes and soothes skin.

head [V-I+ADV/PREP-U2] To **head** in a direction is to travel in that direction.

herbal extract treatment [N-COUNT-U10] A **herbal extract treatment** is a cure that uses natural oils from herbs.

holiday [N-COUNT-U3] A **holiday** is a day when there is no school or work for the purpose of celebrating a special occasion.

honey blonde [ADJ-U8] Hair that is **honey blonde** is blonde with a honey brown tint.

hood-type dryer [N-COUNT-U6] A **hood-type dryer** is a type of hair dryer that covers the top part of the user's head.

hose [N-COUNT-U5] A **hose** is a long tube that transports water.

hours of operation [N PHRASE-U3] **Hours of operation** are the hours during the day when a business is open.

in effect [PREP PHRASE-U3] Something that is **in effect** is currently operating.

ingrown hair [N-COUNT-U13] An **ingrown hair** is a hair that grows into the skin, often causing pain.

interstate [N-COUNT-U2] An **interstate** is a large road that crosses different states and connects major cities.

irritation [N-COUNT-U9] An **irritation** is an uncomfortable reaction to something, often producing red spots when it is a skin irritation.

irritated [ADJ-U13] If something is **irritated**, it is red and inflamed.

itchy [ADJ-U10] If something is **itchy**, it feels uncomfortable and causes you to want to scratch it.

keratin treatment [N-COUNT-U7] A **keratin treatment** is a semi-permanent hair straightening method that involves applying a solution on the hair and activating the chemicals by heat.

landmark [N-COUNT-U2] A **landmark** is a building or feature that is easy to recognize.

lather [N-UNCOUNT-U5] **Lather** is a mass of small white bubbles that forms by mixing soap and water.

leave-in conditioner [N-COUNT-U10] A **leave-in conditioner** is a conditioner that gets applied to the hair and does not get washed out.

light brown [ADJ-U8] Hair that is **light brown** is a pale shade of brown.

lukewarm [ADJ-U5] If something is **lukewarm**, it is slightly warm.

maintain [V-T-U12] To **maintain** something is to take care of it.

mask [N-COUNT-U15] A **mask** is a skincare product that is applied to the face and then washed off to clear pores and refresh the skin.

meet one's needs [V PHRASE-U3] To **meet one's needs** is to satisfy a person's requirements.

merge [V-I-U2] To **merge** is to combine or come together into one.

mind [V-I-U1] To **mind** is to be bothered by something.

mustache [N-COUNT-U9] A **mustache** is hair that covers the upper lip.

nail dryer [N-COUNT-U11] A **nail dryer** is a machine that speeds the drying process for nail polish. Users place their hands inside the machine and wait until the polish dries.

nail plate [N-COUNT-U11] A **nail plate** is the hard part of the nail that is painted during a manicure.

nail polish [N-COUNT-U11] **Nail polish** is a shiny, clear or colored liquid, which is applied to the surface of the nail.

nail polish remover [N-UNCOUNT-U11] **Nail polish remover** is a chemical that dissolves nail polish.

nail technician [N-COUNT-U12] A **nail technician** has the technical knowledge to be able to create beautiful nails.

nape [N-COUNT-U5] The **nape** is the back of the neck.

neutralizer [N-COUNT-U6] A **neutralizer** is a chemical substance that stops the chemicals that create a perm from working.

new hair growth [N PHRASE-U7] **New hair growth** is hair near the scalp that has grown recently.

nick [N-COUNT-U9] A **nick** is a small cut.

no-lye solution [N PHRASE-U7] **No-lye solution** is a type of hair straightening formula that doesn't include a harsh chemical called lye.

non-acetone [ADJ-U11] If something is **non-acetone**, it does not contain a chemical that is commonly used to remove paint from surfaces.

nozzle [N-COUNT-U5] A **nozzle** is an object attached to the end of a tube that directs how the liquid comes out of the tube.

off day [N PHRASE-U3] An **off day** is a day on which a business is closed and its employees do not have to work.

oily [ADJ-U14] When skin is **oily** it is shiny and produces too much oil.

opening [N-COUNT-U4] An **opening** is a time slot that is available in someone's appointment book.

oval [ADJ-U11] An **oval** shape is a shape similar to an egg.

over-processed [ADJ-U10] If something is **over-processed**, it is damaged as a result of hair treatments like dyeing or heat styling.

paraffin wax treatment [N-COUNT-U11] A **paraffin wax treatment** is a service that involves dipping your hands into warm wax, then wrapping the wax-covered hands in a towel. This treatment is used to make the hands soft.

pamper [V-T-U15] To **pamper** is to look after or spoil someone with luxuries.

pat [V-T-U15] To **pat** is to lightly touch someone or something very gently with your hand flat.

patronage [N-UNCOUNT-U3] **Patronage** is the financial support that clients or customers give to a business.

peak hours [N PHRASE-U1] **Peak hours** are the times during the day when a business is very busy.

peel [N-COUNT-U15] A **peel** is a skincare product that is applied to the face and then peeled off. It removes dead skin by pulling it off.

peel [V-I-U12] To **peel** is to lose the top layer of skin.

pencil in [PHRASAL V-U4] To **pencil in** is to schedule an appointment.

perm [N-COUNT-U6] A **perm** is a technique which hairdressers use to curl hair permanently.

perm rods [N-COUNT-U6] **Perm rods** are used to wrap hair around when using chemicals to curl the hair.

platinum [ADJ-U8] Hair that is **platinum** is very pale, almost white.

pluck [V-T-U13] To **pluck** something is to pull something out from somewhere.

pore [N-COUNT-U14] A **pore** is a tiny opening in the skin.

prepare [V-T-U11] To **prepare** something is to make it ready to use.

procedure [N-COUNT-U7] A **procedure** is the series of steps or actions in order to make something happen.

protective gloves [N-COUNT-U6] **Protective gloves** are hand coverings used to keep the hands dry and prevent them from being damaged.

purple-black [ADJ-U8] Hair that is **purple-black** is dark black with purple tones in it.

quarter-sized [ADJ-U5] If something is **quarter-sized**, it is the same amount and shape as a quarter coin.

ramp [N-COUNT-U2] A **ramp** is a road which cars use to drive onto a major road.

rash [N-COUNT-U14] A **rash** is an area of skin that red is with raised spots.

receptionist [N-COUNT-U4] A **receptionist** is someone who answers phones, greets visitors and initially deals with clients.

redhead [N-COUNT-U8] A **redhead** is a person with red hair.

regimen [N-COUNT-U14] A **regimen** is a plan for treating a condition.

regular hours [N-PHRASE-U3] **Regular hours** are the hours when a business is usually open.

remove [V-T-U11] To **remove** nail polish means to take it off.

repeat client [N-COUNT-U1] A **repeat client** is someone who visits the same business more than once.

ridge [N-COUNT-U11] A **ridge** is a bump or imperfection on an otherwise flat surface.

rod [N-COUNT-U6] A **rod** is a thin and flexible piece of plastic or metal that is used to create a curl shape in hair.

rule book [N-COUNT-U3] A **rule book** contains the rules of an organization, job or game.

salon [N-COUNT-U1] A **salon** is the place where beauty products get applied and a person can receive massages or other relaxing therapies.

salon staff [N-PHRASE-U3] **Salon staff** are the people that work in a salon.

saturate [V-T-U5] To **saturate** something is to make something totally wet.

scalp [N-COUNT-U10] The **scalp** is the skin covering the top of the human head.

scratch [V-I-U12] To **scratch** something is to mark the surface of something, usually with something sharp or rough.

scrub [N-COUNT-U15] A **scrub** is a skincare product that is made of a coarse material.

seal [N-COUNT-U12] A **seal** is something that keeps water or air from entering an object.

sensitive skin [N PHRASE-U15] **Sensitive skin** is skin that can easily react badly to certain products and conditions.

serum [N-COUNT-U7] A **serum** is a thick liquid that has a high amount of substances that perform a specific function, like straightening hair.

shampoo [N-COUNT-U5] **Shampoo** is the liquid soap-based substance we use to wash hair.

shampoo chair [N-COUNT-U5] A **shampoo chair** is a seat that is specially designed for giving clients a professional shampoo. It has an adjustable height and reclines.

shape [V-T-U11] To **shape** is to give something a particular shape or form.

sharp [ADJ-U9] When someone is **sharp**, he or she is well groomed.

shaving brush [N-COUNT-U9] A **shaving brush** is a brush for spreading soap or shaving cream over the face when you shave.

shaving cream [N-UNCOUNT-U9] **Shaving cream** is a kind of cream that is put on a person's face or body before shaving.

shrink [V-I-U12] To **shrink** is to become smaller.

sign-in sheet [N-COUNT-U1] A **sign-in sheet** is a piece of paper on which people write their name to let the staff know that they've arrived.

skincare [N-UNCOUNT-U14] **Skincare** refers to things that a person does to improve the condition of the skin.

slough [V-T-U15] To **slough** something is to rub away a layer.

smooth [ADJ-U7] If something is **smooth**, it has a surface without lumps or imperfections.

smudge [V-T-U12] To **smudge** something is to rub something and make it blurry or ruin its surface.

split end [N-COUNT-U10] A **split end** is the tip of a strand of hair that has divided due to dryness or overprocessing.

square [ADJ-U11] **Square** means having four equal length sides and right-angled corners.

squoval [ADJ-U11] **Squoval** means having a shape with four rounded corners.

steam [V-T-U15] To **steam** something is to expose it to hot water vapor.

straight razor [N-COUNT-U9] A **straight razor** is a type of razor with one long blade that folds out from the handle.

strip [N-COUNT-U13] A **strip** is a long and narrow piece of material.

stylist [N-COUNT-U4] A **stylist** is a person whose job it is to creatively design the look of someone or something.

styptic pencil [N-COUNT-U9] A **styptic pencil** is a tool that is used to treat cuts caused by shaving.

summer look [N-PHRASE-U3] A **summer look** is a particular appearance someone has during the summer months.

sun spot [N-COUNT-U14] A **sun spot** is an area of the skin that is darker than the rest of the skin. This is caused by exposure to the sun.

sunscreen [N-UNCOUNT-U14] **Sunscreen** is a substance that protects the skin from the sun's rays.

tail comb [N-COUNT-U6] A **tail comb** is a type of comb with a thin and pointed handle which is often used to divide the hair into different sections.

thermal reconditioning [N-UNCOUNT-U7] **Thermal reconditioning** is a permanent hair straightening method that involves applying a chemical solution to the hair and activating the chemicals by heat.

thinning hair [N-UNCOUNT-U10] **Thinning hair** is a condition in which hair volume on the head decreases due to age or other circumstances.

threading [N-UNCOUNT-U13] **Threading** is the process of removing hair using a twisted piece of thread to pull hair from the skin.

toner [N-COUNT-U15] A **toner** is a liquid that reduces oiliness and makes the skin firm.

topcoat [N-COUNT-U12] A **topcoat** is the last layer of paint, varnish or polish put on a surface.

towel dry [V-T-U5] To **towel dry** something is to take away all of something's wetness by rubbing it with a towel.

treatment [N-UNCOUNT-U15] A beauty **treatment** is a service offered to people at a salon.

tuck in [Phrasal V-U5] To **tuck in** something is to fit it snugly into something else.

turn [V-I-U2] To **turn** is to move in a different direction.

tweezers [N-UNCOUNT-U13] **Tweezers** are a tool with two metal pieces that are connected on one end. They are used to grab small objects.

twist [V-T-U13] To **twist** something is to turn and bend something.

t-zone [N-COUNT-U14] The **t-zone** is the area of the face including the forehead and nose.

volume-boosting [ADJ-U10] A hair product that is **volume-boosting** makes hair look thicker.

wait time [N PHRASE-U1] A **wait time** is the length of a time a person has to wait before he or she can see someone.

waiting area [N-COUNT-U1] A **waiting area** is a place where people wait.

walk-ins [N-COUNT-U1] **Walk-ins** are people who visit a business without making an appointment.

waxing [N-COUNT-U13] **Waxing** is the process of removing hair by applying wax to the skin, applying a strip over the wax, and quickly pulling the strip off.

weekday [N-COUNT-U3] A **weekday** is a day of the week from Monday to Friday.

weekend [N-COUNT-U4] A **weekend** is the last two days of the week.

wet shave [N-COUNT-U9] A **wet shave** is a type of shave that is done using shaving cream.

work week [N-UNCOUNT-U4] A **work week** is the hours or days that are worked during a week.

wrap [V-T-U5] To **wrap** something is to cover it with a material.

wrinkle [N-COUNT-U14] A **wrinkle** is a fold in a smooth surface.

Beauty Salon

Book 3

Jenny Dooley
Virginia Evans

Express Publishing

Table of Contents

complimentary robe

promotion

discount

-50 %

Get ready!

1 Before you read the passage, talk about these questions.

1 Do you think visiting a beauty salon is expensive?

2 What sort of promotions do beauty salons in your town offer?

Reading

2 Read this flyer from a beauty salon. Then, mark the following statements as true (T) or false (F).

1 ___ New clients are eligible for a twenty-five percent discount on the Cherry Blossom package.

2 ___ The salon is offering featured products at half price this week.

3 ___ The most affordable spa weekend package is $700.

Vocabulary

3 Read the sentence and choose the correct word.

1 The store manager ran a **promotion / pricing** to attract new clients.

2 The Johnson family received a 25% **discount / package** when they took advantage of the salon's promotion.

3 The store's **featured products / reduced rates** are at the front of the store to encourage clients to buy them.

4 The prices for the salon's nail services **start at / range from** $45 to $200.

4 Fill in the blanks with the correct words and phrases from the word bank.

WORD BANK

specials   complimentary   applies to
seasonal   pricing   start at

1 Julian called the salon about their _____ so he would know how much money to bring with him.

2 The new client deal only _____ clients who have not visited the salon before.

3 The salon offers a(n) _____ promotion in which clients can enjoy treatments with fresh herbs found only at that time of year.

4 The salon advertises its weekly _____ in the local newspaper every Tuesday.

5 The salon's prices _____ $200, but there are many services that are much more expensive.

6 Regina didn't pay for the massage because it was _____.

Bella Salon
Springtime Promotions

This spring, it doesn't have to cost you a fortune to look good. Take advantage of the **specials** at Bella Salon for great deals on a number of our services.

March Promotions

For the entire month of March, get a trim, shampoo, & **blow-dry** for the price of just a trim (you must mention this promotion to receive this special offer).

Get 25% off if you are a new client (**reduced rate** does not **apply to** spa services).

50% **discount** off this week's **featured products** from our salon shop, which include:
↦ Shimmer and Glow Cosmetics
↦ Vita Shampoos and Conditioners
↦ OMG Nail Polishes

Visit our website today, for a complete list of this week's featured products and special offers.

Spa Packages

Our spa **packages start at** $200 and include a **complimentary robe** for your day at the spa. Receive 10% off immediately when you treat yourself to our special **seasonal** spa package, the Cherry Blossom. This package includes a facial, body scrub and body oil massage.

Looking for springtime relaxation and **rejuvenation**? Then, arrange a spa weekend with Bella Salon today. Spa weekends **range from** $700 to $1500 per person. Visit our website or call today for **pricing**.

5 🎧 Listen and read the flyer from a beauty salon again. Why is it a good idea to have a haircut at Bella Salon in March?

Listening

6 🎧 Listen to a conversation between a caller and a receptionist. Choose the correct answers.

1 The woman calls the salon in order to _____ .
   A cancel her hair appointment
   B learn the cost of services at the salon
   C ask for a discount on a haircut
   D make an appointment for a massage

2 What can be inferred about the caller?
   A she is a regular at the salon
   B she has never had a massage before
   C her friends are clients at the salon
   D her schedule is full until next week

7 🎧 Listen again and complete the conversation.

Caller:	Hello, could you tell me about this month's promotions?
Receptionist:	Well, you can get a trim, **1** _____ _____ _____ - _____ all for $45. It's part of our springtime promotion.
Caller:	Now that's a good price. Do you have any other **2** _____?
Receptionist:	Yes. Let me ask you. Have you ever visited Bella Salon before?
Caller:	No, I haven't. But my friends have and they told me good things about it.
Receptionist:	Since that's the case, you can also get an additional 25% **3** _____ your first visit.
Caller:	That's a huge **4** _____ . Maybe I'll sign up for a massage while I'm at it.
Receptionist:	Unfortunately, the new client discount doesn't include **5** _____ _____ .
Caller:	That's too bad. Anyway, how do I **6** _____ _____ of these great offers?
Receptionist:	When you come in, mention the promotions I just told you about.

Speaking

8 With a partner, act out the roles below based on Task 7. Then, switch roles.

Student A: You are a receptionist at the Bella Salon. Talk to Student B about:
● the price of services
● what discounts or specials are available to him or her
● how he or she can receive the discounts

Student B: You are a caller interested in services at the Bella Salon. Tell Student A what service you are interested in. Then, ask questions to find out about:
● the prices for that service
● any promotions
● how to get the special prices

Writing

9 You are a salon owner. Use the flyer and the conversation from Task 8 to create a flyer for a promotion at your salon. Include:
● The details of the promotion
● The conditions of the promotion

pricing

Shampoo & Blow dry $ 35.00
Trim $12.00-$15.00
Permanent Color $35.00
Hair Treatments $15.00-45.00

2 How will you pay?

credit cards

personal check

coupons

cash

gift certificate

Bella Salon FAQ

Many clients who visit us are unfamiliar with salon **payment procedures**. Here are answers to some frequently asked questions.

What methods of payment are accepted?

The Bella Salon accepts most **methods of payment**, including all major **credit cards, debit cards, personal checks** and **cash**.

How do I use a gift certificate?

When you arrive, please notify the receptionist that you intend to pay by **gift certificate**. Unfortunately, we cannot accept or **refund expired** gift certificates. Gift certificates are good for up to one year after purchase and any charges that exceed the total listed on the gift certificate will appear on a separate **bill**.

How much should I tip?

The standard salon **tip** is between 15% and 20% of your treatment cost (before **tax**). Please give any tips in cash directly to your stylist, nail technician or makeup artist.

Where can I find Bella Salon coupons?

Discount coupons for the Bella Salon are available in the Sunday newspaper and are **valid** for between one week and one month, depending on the promotion.

Please note that nail technicians will ask for payment before starting your manicure. This is to avoid ruining your nails.

Get ready!

1 Before you read the passage, talk about these questions.

1 How do people normally pay for services and products nowadays?

2 Would you prefer to receive a gift certificate instead of a gift? Why/Why not?

Reading

2 Read the web page. Then, choose the right answers.

1 What is the main topic of the web page?

A to train employees how to accept different methods of payment

B to give information about different forms of payment used in the salon

C to encourage clients to buy gift certificates

D to inform clients about the typical cost of a salon visit

2 What is true about gift certificates?

A They are valid for a limited amount of time.

B Old certificates can be exchanged for cash.

C All salon costs must be covered by the certificate.

D The stylist needs to know that a client plans to use a gift certificate.

3 What can be inferred about Bella Salon?

A It does not honor gift certificates.

B It charges an extra fee to people who pay by check.

C It limits how many coupons clients can use per visit.

D It does not include the tip in the total bill.

Vocabulary

3 Read the sentences and choose the correct meaning of the underlined word.

1 Henry charged the airline ticket to his credit card.

A a plastic card that customers use to buy goods or services and pay for them later

B a plastic card that allows someone to take cash from his/her bank account to pay for goods

C a plastic card that lets a person pay less for something or receive something for free

2 Meghan used the gift certificate she received for her birthday to buy clothes in the store.

A money that the government charges in order to pay for services and projects for the public

B a small amount of extra money that customers give to a person who has provided a service

C a document issued from a business that is worth a certain sum of money at that business

3 Andrea collected coupons in order to save money on her grocery bill.

A pieces of paper which are filled out by users and that direct banks to take money from the user's account

B pieces of paper issued by a store that gives customers a reduced price on specific items

C pieces of paper that look like receipts.

4 **Write a word that is similar in meaning to the underlined part.**

1 Crystal did not have enough <u>money that is made up of bills and coins</u> to cover her tab and had to borrow from her friend.   _ a _ h

2 The manager taught the new employee about the <u>typical and correct ways of paying</u> at the company.
p _ y _ _ n _   _ r _ c _ _ u r _ _

3 Don't forget to redeem your gift certificate before <u>it is no longer valid</u> at the end of the year.   _ _ p i _ e _

4 The store does not give <u>an amount of money back</u> if thirty days or more have passed after the purchase date.
a   r _ _ u _ d

5 🎧 **Listen and read the web page again. What happens when a client spends more than the gift certificate is worth?**

Listening

6 🎧 **Listen to a conversation between a client and a cashier at Bella Salon. Mark the following statements as true (T) or false (F).**

1 __ The woman uses a debit card to pay for her salon bill.

2 __ The final total includes the tip for the salon worker.

3 __ The woman can leave as much as she wants for the tip.

7 🎧 **Listen again and complete the conversation.**

Client: Hello. Can I pay here?

Cashier: Of course. I'll ring you up. I have you down for a pedicure with a twenty minute leg and foot massage. Is that correct?

Client: That's right.

Cashier: Okay. The total is $50. How would you like to **1** _____ ?

Client: I forgot my debit **2** _____ at home, so I'm hoping you **3** _____ _____ .

Cashier: Yes. Just write it out to Bella Salon.

Client: Should I include the tip in the **4** _____ ?

Cashier: Actually, you should give the tip **5** _____ to the pedicurist.

Client: Okay. How much do most people usually **6** _____ ?

Cashier: Between 15% and 20% of the **7** _____ before tax. But it's entirely at your discretion .

Speaking

8 **With a partner, act out the roles below based on Task 7. Then, switch roles.**

USE LANGUAGE SUCH AS:

How would you like to pay?

I'm hoping you …

How much do most people usually tip?

Student A: You are a cashier at Bella Salon. Confirm which services Student B had. Then, talk about:
● the total
● how he or she will pay the bill
● the tipping policy at the salon

Student B: You are a client at the Bella Salon. Confirm the services you used with Student A, then, respond to his or her questions.

Writing

9 **You are a salon manager. Use the web page and the conversation from Task 8 to write an employee memo about payment methods. Include:**

● The payment methods accepted at the salon

● How to deal with coupons and gift certificates

● How to handle tips

retouch

Ask a Stylist

Lori Sheldon of the Bella Salon

What's the difference between permanent and semi-permanent hair color?

Semi-permanent dye **fades** away after 4-6 weeks. As it doesn't chemically alter the color of the hair, it can't be used for **lightening** and may not cover grays. The advantage is that **semi-permanent** color can be frequently reapplied without **damaging** the hair.

Permanent dye changes the actual color of the hair, allowing clients to select from a wider color **palette** and to **conceal** grays. It's advisable to **retouch** just the roots, as each additional application increases damage to the hair. The only way to remove permanent hair color is to completely let it **grow out**, then cut it.

How can I minimize damage to my hair from color treatments?

Ask your stylist about the chemicals in the dyes that the salon uses. You want to avoid products that have a high ammonia content and lack conditioning ingredients.

What is a patch test?

Be sure to visit your salon 48 hours prior to your appointment for a **patch test**. Your stylist will clean a small area of skin, usually on the inside of your elbow, and apply a **test solution** of dye. Provided that you don't experience an **allergic reaction**, you're good to go!

Get ready!

1 **Before you read the passage, talk about these questions.**

1 What are some reasons to dye your hair at the salon rather than at home?

2 How do people maintain their colored hair?

Reading

2 **Read the column from a trade magazine. Then, mark the following statements as true (T) or false (F).**

1 __ Regular application of semi-permanent dye causes damage to hair.

2 __ Permanent dye is better for concealing grays than semi-permanent dye.

3 __ A patch test is typically conducted by the salon two days before dyeing.

Vocabulary

3 **Read the sentence pair. Choose where the words best fit the blanks.**

1 **test solution / allergic reaction**

The stylist did a test on her client's skin because some people have a(n) _____ to certain colors.

Jean mixed the _____ and applied it to the inside of the client's elbow.

2 **conceal / lighten**

It is quite easy to _____ gray hair with a permanent dye.

Olivia used a hair color to _____ her hair.

3 **permanent / semi-permanent**

The _____ dye damaged Rosa's hair and she could not dye it again until new hair grew.

Alicia reapplied _____ dye to her hair every two weeks to keep the color from fading.

lighten

grow out

fade

4 Check (✓) the sentence that uses the underlined part correctly.

1 __ **A** The color of my hair <u>fades</u> when I stay in the sun too often.

__ **B** Sarah wants her hair to <u>grow out</u> so she curls it every day.

2 __ **A** Ted gave his client a <u>patch test</u> soon after coloring her hair.

__ **B** Julie chose the new color for her hair from the <u>palette</u> at the salon.

3 __ **A** Petra <u>retouched</u> her roots when they started to grow out.

__ **B** Max was pleased when the dye <u>damaged</u> his hair.

5 🎧 Listen and read the column from a trade magazine again. What should you try to avoid when coloring hair?

Listening

6 🎧 Listen to a conversation between a client and a colorist at a salon. Choose the correct answers.

1 What happens during the conversation?

A The man dyes his hair.

B The man has an allergic reaction.

C The colorist carries out a patch test.

D The colorist changes the man's appointment.

2 What is true about the man's previous dye job?

A It damaged his hair.

B It concealed his gray hair.

C It involved permanent hair dye.

D It faded away fast.

7 🎧 Listen again and complete the conversation.

Colorist:	Have you ever had a **1** _____ _____ before, Matt?
Client:	Yes, I had one at my old hairdresser's.
Colorist:	So, you've had your hair **2** _____ before?
Client:	Yes, but I wasn't happy with the results.
Colorist:	What was the problem?
Client:	The color **3** _____ too quickly.
Colorist:	Sounds like your hairdresser used **4** _____ - _____ dye. If you want lasting results, let's go with a permanent color.
Client:	Sounds great.
Colorist:	Now, can I have you roll up your sleeve, please?
Client:	Sure.
Colorist:	Now, I've applied the **5** _____ _____ . Call us immediately if your **6** _____ reacts. Assuming it doesn't, I'll see you on Friday.

Speaking

8 With a partner, act out the roles below based on Task 7. Then, switch roles.

USE LANGUAGE SUCH AS:

Have you ever had a patch test before?

What was the problem?

Sounds like your hairdresser used …

Student A: You are a colorist at the Bella Salon. Talk to Student B about:

- his or her problems with past dye jobs
- your solution to the problem
- the patch test

Student B: You are a client at Bella Salon and you are receiving a patch test before a dye job. Respond to Student A's questions. Also, ask Student A about the patch test.

Writing

9 You are a writer for a beauty magazine. Use the column and the conversation from Task 8 to write an article about successfully coloring hair. Include:

- The pros and cons of different types of dyes
- The importance of a patch test

9

Don't Try These at Home

Double Process Color

Double process color involves **bleaching** the hair, then adding dye to it. This procedure is commonly used when lightening the **base color** by two or more shades. Unlike **single process color**, which is common in **home hair color kits**, double process color is best left to professionals to avoid overprocessing the hair.

Highlights & Lowlights

Highlights and **lowlights** add dimension to your hair color by creating areas that are lighter and darker than the rest of your hair. While you can give yourself highlights at home, a professional can give you the best results with either a **cap highlight** or **foil highlight**. The cap highlight is suitable for clients seeking a uniform color. Though the foil highlight is typically more expensive, it is preferable when trying for **two-toned** or multi-colored hair.

 highlights
 foil highlight
 lowlights

Corrective Color

If you use a home coloring kit and end up with a color you aren't happy with, don't try to fix the **botched** dye job yourself, you'll only make it worse. Instead, consult a professional colorist, who has the expertise to fix it without further damaging your hair.

Get ready!

1 Before you read the passage, talk about these questions.

1 What are some of the problems that may occur from coloring hair yourself?

2 What are some techniques that only professional colorists can do?

Reading

2 Read the article from a magazine. Then, choose the correct answers.

1 What is the main topic of the article?

A how to use home hair color kits

B the jobs that professional colorists should do

C problems with professional dye jobs

D how to get professional results at home

2 What is true about single process color?

A It involves bleaching the hair.

B It is not available in salons.

C It is more damaging than double process color.

D It is safe for non-professionals to use.

3 According to the article, what is an advantage of foil highlights?

A They involve a single process.

B They give all of the hair single color.

C They create areas with different colors.

D They are an affordable alternative to cap highlights.

Vocabulary

3 Choose the word that is closest in meaning to the underlined part.

1 Melissa made an appointment for sections of her hair to be made a darker color than the rest.

A lowlights   B highlights

C base color

2 Betty had tried hair dye products to use at home, but she prefers her professional colorist to do it.

A cap highlights   B double

C home hair color kits   process color

3 The stylist advised Gwen against drastically changing her natural color of hair.

A single process color   B base color

C foil highlights

4 Match the words (1-6) with the definitions (A-F).

1 __ corrective   4 __ botched

2 __ two-toned   5 __ bleach

3 __ highlight   6 __ single process color

A spoiled because of a mistake

B a hair color method that involves coloring all of the hair one color

C to remove color from something

D an area of the hair that is lighter than the rest of the hair

E fixes or improves

F having two different colors or shades

5 🎧 **Listen and read the article from a magazine again. Which technique would someone choose to dye their hair different shades?**

Listening

6 🎧 **Listen to a conversation between a client and a colorist at a salon. Choose the correct answers.**

1   What service does the colorist suggest?
   - **A**   highlights
   - **B**   double process color
   - **C**   single process color
   - **D**   home hair color kit

2   What is true about the client?
   - **A**   She bleached her hair at home.
   - **B**   She used a home hair color kit.
   - **C**   She has dark hair.
   - **D**   She has damaged hair.

7 🎧 **Listen again and complete the conversation.**

Colorist:	Why don't you tell me what you want to have done today?
Client:	I want to **1**_____ _____ .
Colorist:	Oh, then I'm glad you came to see me.
Client:	What do you mean?
Colorist:	You have very **2**_____ _____ . Trying to lighten it at home could cause terrible damage .
Client:	I did think about doing it at home. There are plenty of **3**_____ _____ _____ _____ .
Colorist:	Yes, but it would be hard to achieve the results you want with a home kit.
Client:	Why is that?
Colorist:	For the color you want, you need **4**_____ _____ _____ .
Client:	And I can't do that at home?
Colorist:	I wouldn't recommend it. Besides, most home kits are **5**_____ _____ _____ .

Speaking

8 **With a partner, act out the roles below based on Task 7. Then, switch roles.**

USE LANGUAGE SUCH AS:

I want …

Oh, then I'm glad you came to see me.

For the color you want, you need …

Student A: You are a colorist at Bella Salon. Ask Student B what service they want. Then, explain why it is best to leave that service to a professional, being sure to mention:

- the potential harmful effects of using a home color kit for the service Student A wants
- why a professional is better suited to perform the service

Student B: You are a client at Bella Salon. Tell Student A what hair color service you want, choosing between:

- coloring your hair more than two shades lighter than your base color
- getting highlights or lowlights
- getting a previous dye job corrected

Writing

9 **You are an online beauty expert. Use the article and the conversation from Task 8 to write about why clients should choose a professional colorist over a home hair color kit. Include:**

- Why coloring hair is best left to the professionals
- What different coloring techniques there are

home hair color kit

bleach

5 Curly hair

curl pattern

frayed

air dry

diffuser

Get ready!

❶ Before you read the passage, talk about these questions.

1 What are some hair problems that people with curly hair may have?

2 In your opinion, which is easier to take care of; curly or straight hair?

Reading

❷ Read this pamphlet from a beauty salon. Then, mark the following statements as true (T) or false (F).

1 __ The salon cuts curly hair with a razor when the hair is dry.

2 __ A blow dryer without a diffuser increases frizz.

3 __ Humidity makes it harder to manage curly hair.

Vocabulary

❸ Choose the correct word pair to fill the blanks.

1 Rebecca didn't have time to ____ her hair, so she used a blow dryer with a ____ .
   A scrunch - absorb
   B air dry - diffuser
   C repel - dry cut

2 Jesse's hair is never ____ when the ____ in the city rises.
   A damp - diffuser
   B frayed - silicone
   C manageable - humidity

3 Allison ____ her hair in her hands, then applied a product that contained ____ to avoid frizziness.
   A scrunched - silicone
   B repelled - curl patterns
   C absorbed - diffusers

Bella Salon: Caring for Curly Hair

The stylists at Bella Salon are specially trained in cutting and styling curly hair. We *always* **dry cut** curly hair in order to create a style that suits your natural **curl pattern**. Also, you'll never catch one of our stylists using a razor on curly hair, which leaves the ends of the hair **frayed**.

Home Care

The secret to **manageable** curly hair is moisture. Use conditioner every day and apply a leave-in conditioner once a week. Remember, it is impossible to moisturize curly hair too much.

Once you're out of the shower, don't towel-dry your hair. Instead, use paper towels to **absorb** excess moisture. Then, allow the hair to **air dry**, making sure not to touch or **scrunch** the hair while it's still **damp**. If you're short on time, select a blow dryer with a **diffuser** attachment, as diffusers **enhance** curls and decrease the likelihood of frizz.

Humidity

Humidity can turn a head of beautiful curls into a frizzy mess. So it's advisable to keep a range of products on hand on humid days. Look for an anti-frizz serum containing **silicone**, which **repels** moisture and shields your hair from heat. There are many products that are specifically designed for curly hair, including Bella Salon's Corkscrew line.

❹ Fill in the blanks with the correct words and phrases from the word bank.

WOrd BANK

repels   absorb   damp
curl pattern   dry cut

1 Elaine asked the stylist not to wet her hair because she wanted a _____ .

2 Will used a sponge to _____ the spilt water.

3 After walking in the rain, Heather's hair felt _____ and lifeless.

4 The spray _____ moisture, but it needs to be reapplied again after an hour.

5 Lisa and Wanda both have curly hair, but each has a distinct _____ .

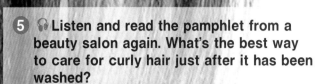

5 🎧 **Listen and read the pamphlet from a beauty salon again. What's the best way to care for curly hair just after it has been washed?**

Listening

6 🎧 **Listen to a conversation between a stylist and a client. Choose the correct answers.**

1 What advice does the stylist give the woman?

   A use anti-frizz products

   B get a short haircut

   C dry the hair with paper towels

   D use a diffuser attachment

2 Which part of the woman's hair routine likely contributes to her unruly hair?

   A She uses a leave-in conditioner too often.

   B She conditions her hair daily.

   C She dries her hair with a blow dryer.

   D She shampoos her hair every day.

7 🎧 **Listen again and complete the conversation.**

Stylist: Tell me, what's your typical **1** _____ _____?

Client: I use shampoo and conditioner every day. And I **2** _____ - _____ it when I get out of the shower.

Stylist: It's good that you **3** _____ your hair every day. That helps keep it healthy.

Client: Then, why is it that my hair still feels so dry?

Stylist: You probably need to start using a **4** _____ - _____ conditioner at least once a week. Curly hair needs to be moisturized often.

Client: I can do that.

Stylist: Also, you should stop using your blow dryer. Blow drying actually causes **5** _____ .

Client: So, what should I do instead? I hate leaving the house with wet hair.

Stylist: If you can't air dry your hair, use a blow dryer that has a **6** _____ attachment.

Client: I'll try that. Thanks for the tips!

Speaking

8 **With a partner, act out the roles below based on Task 7. Then, switch roles.**

USE LANGUAGE SUCH AS:

Tell me, what's your typical hair routine?

It's good that you …

Also, you should …

Student A: You are a stylist at Bella Salon. Ask Student B about his or her typical hair routine. Then, give advice about caring for his or her hair, being sure to mention:

● a part of the his or her routine that is good, if possible

● what habits are bad for his or her hair

Student B: You are a client with curly hair. Tell Student A your typical hair routine. Then, respond to his or her questions and advice for caring for your hair.

Writing

9 **You are a stylist at a salon. Use the passage and the conversation from Task 8 to write a memo to the stylists about how to care for curly hair. Include:**

● The appropriate way to cut curly hair

● Advice to give clients with curly hair

● Products that reduce frizz

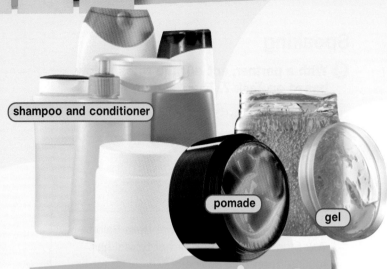

shampoo and conditioner

pomade

gel

Product Reviews

Compiled by: Emily Withers

In Style Mousse
★★★☆☆

This volumizing **mousse** is great for people with fine hair. However, some users found that it leaves a greasy **film** on hair.

Hold It! Spritz
★★★★☆

Hold It! **spritzes** and **hairsprays** have been a favorite amongst industry professionals for years, and now consumers are finding out why. These products help hold styles and never make hair feel stiff. The downside? They tend to be pricey.

All Nature Clarifying Shampoo
★★★★★

The **mild** cleansing agents in this **lightweight shampoo** remove product **buildup** and leave your hair feeling clean and soft. Since it's

fragrance-free, it's great for people with sensitive skin and scalp.

NYC Forever Hair Gel
★★★☆☆

This **hair gel** claims to give users a more natural look without making hair too stiff. For people with coarse hair, it is perfect for creating long-lasting styles. However, users with fine hair have found that this gel doesn't hold styles for very long.

Shine Pomade
★★★★☆

Prevent unruly hair and **nourish** your locks with Shine **Pomade**. Unlike other pomades, this one doesn't make hair greasy and has a pleasant fragrance. However, if you put too much of this on, it will weigh down your hair and make it appear limp.

Get ready!

1 **Before you read the passage, talk about these questions.**

1 What are some common hair problems that people have?

2 What are the different hair products that people use?

Reading

2 **Read these reviews from a beauty magazine. Then, mark the following statements as true (T) or false (F).**

1 __ People with skin problems will have no complaints about the clarifying shampoo.

2 __ The hair gel is not recommended for people with fine hair.

3 __ Hold It! Spritz is only available to salon professionals.

Vocabulary

3 **Check (✓) the sentence that uses the underlined part correctly.**

1 __ A Karla likes the lime smell of the fragrance-free lotion.

__ B After removing the buildup, Janie's hair was easier to manage.

2 __ A The clarifying shampoo made Greg's hair transparent.

__ B Hannah uses a spritz to make her hair stay in place.

3 __ A Rick's hair was easier to control after he spread the pomade on it.

__ B This new, lightweight shampoo will add buildup to your hair.

4 __ A The vitamins in the product help nourish hair.

__ B The mild film will leave your hair feeling clean and soft.

4 **Write a word that is similar in meaning to the underlined part.**

1 Jake used a foam hair product to help his hair appear thicker. _ o _ s _ e

2 Patricia has sensitive skin, so she always buys cosmetics and hair products that are gentle and less likely to cause side effects. _ i l _

3 Alex uses a thick, spreadable hair product that holds hair in place to style his hair. _ a _ _   _ _ l

4 Emily holds her breath when she uses an aerosol hair product that holds hair in place because she doesn't like to inhale the fumes. h _ _ r s _ r _ _

5 🎧 Listen and read the reviews from a beauty magazine again. Which product should someone avoid if their hair type is fine?

Listening

6 🎧 Listen to a conversation between a client and a stylist. Choose the correct answers.

1 What are the speakers mostly talking about?

    A the type of haircut that the woman wants

    B recommendations for styling products

    C the kinds of products that the stylist uses

    D which products are on sale at the salon

2 According to the stylist, why might the hair gel not work for the woman?

    A It doesn't suit her hair type.

    B She has used mousse for too long.

    C Her hair is too coarse.

    D She does not use enough gel.

7 🎧 Listen again and complete the conversation.

Client:	I have a lot of trouble styling my hair. Can you **1** _____ some products for me to use?
Stylist:	Sure. What exactly is the problem?
Client:	Well, I use hair gel to style my hair, but it never **2** _____ for very long.
Stylist:	I think I know what the problem is.
Client:	What is it?
Stylist:	Some hair gels are better-suited for people with **3** _____ _____ . You might want to try a different brand. Or you can try **4** _____ instead.
Client:	I've never used mousse before. How would that help?
Stylist:	Well, you'll see that it gives more **5** _____ that gel does.
Client:	That sounds really great. Is there a brand you recommend?
Stylist:	There are several. Why don't you **6** _____ _____ _____ at the ones we sell here at the salon? Then, I can tell you more about them.
Client:	Great idea. Thanks a lot.

Speaking

8 With a partner, act out the roles below based on Task 7. Then, switch roles.

USE LANGUAGE SUCH AS:

Can you recommend some products for me to use?

What exactly is the problem?

I use …, but it …

Student A: You are a stylist at Bella Salon. Find out what styling product Student B uses and then:

● ask what problems he or she has with that product

● explain possible reasons why the product doesn't work

● recommend a product that might work for Student A

Student B: You are a client at a salon. Tell Student A which styling product you use and what problem you have with that product. Then, ask Student A for recommendations on a good styling product for you.

Writing

9 You are the advice columnist at a fashion magazine. Use the reviews and the conversation from Task 8 to write a response to a reader with hair issues. Include:

● The type of hair the reader has

● Suitable products for this hair type

● Styling tips

15

shaving brush

mustache scissors

shaving bowl

beard trimmer

sideburns

Get ready!

1 Before you read the passage, talk about these questions.

1 In what ways do men groom themselves?

2 What tools are used in men's grooming?

Reading

2 Read the letter from a beauty supply company. Then, choose the right answers.

1 What is the letter about?

   A a problem with the client's request

   B new items on offer by the company

   C a confirmation of the client's order

   D information about available discounts

2 What is NOT true about Hermosa Beauty Supply?

   A It has never supplied Mr Taylor's salon.

   B It is promoting products for men.

   C It is offering an incentive to buy the products.

   D It is targeting clients who have done business with them before.

3 How is Hermosa Beauty Supply's electric razor different from other electric razors?

   A It uses new technology.

   B It does not require water to function.

   C It is completely waterproof.

   D It has self-sharpening blades.

Vocabulary

3 Read the sentence and choose the correct word or phrase.

1 Paul filled the **shaving bowl / mustache wax** with shaving cream.

2 The barber sharpened his razor with a **beard trimmer / hanging strop**.

3 Jeff only buys **shaving brushes / mustache scissors** that are made of natural hair.

4 Grace is careful not to cut herself with the **wax / blade**.

Mr. Collin Taylor
Bella Salon
3278 Wilshire Blvd.
Los Angeles, CA 90076

Dear Mr. Taylor,
           September 25

Hermosa Beauty Supply is pleased to announce the launch of our new men's **grooming** line. As a longtime client, we hope that you will consider the following products for your salon.

Straight Razor: Our straight razor is ideal for grooming **sideburns**. It boasts an easy-to-change **blade** that folds neatly into an ebony handle (a hanging **strop** is included with purchase).

Electric Razor: You won't find another electric razor with our one-of-a-kind triple-razor action. This state-of-the-art razor gives the **closest dry shave** on the market. In fact, testing demonstrated that our razor offers a closer shave than our competitors.

Beard Trimmer: Beard maintenance has never been easier, thanks to our **self-sharpening blades**, guaranteed to leave facial hair looking well-groomed.

Mustache care: Available in a convenient stick format, our **mustache wax** tames the most unruly hair. Our **mustache scissors** are made from stainless steel and have enlarged finger holes for precision grooming.

Nose and ear hair trimmer: Our trimmer is equipped with a built-in spotlight and a mini-vacuum to keep your work area clean.

Shaving bowl: Add a personal touch with our chrome shaving bowls, which can be monogrammed with your salon's initials.

Shaving brush: All our shaving brushes are handmade and crafted from 100% natural badger hair.

Place your order today and receive a free gift with your purchase!

Barbara Horton
Sales Representative, Hermosa Beauty Supply

4 Check (✓) the sentence that uses the underlined part correctly.

1 __ **A** Kevin uses <u>mustache wax</u> to help his facial hair appear tidy and professional.

   __ **B** Jacob cleaned the razor with a <u>self-sharpening</u> blade.

2 __ **A** William shaved his moustache off with the <u>mustache scissors</u>.

   __ **B** The barber made sure that Martin's <u>sideburns</u> were even on each side.

3 __ **A** Mike buys a lot of <u>grooming</u> products to throw away.

   __ **B** Bart gets such a close <u>shave</u> from his new razor that his chin is now completely smooth.

5 🎧 **Listen and read the letter from a beauty supply company again. What did the company's research discover about their electric razor?**

Listening

6 🎧 **Listen to a conversation between a barbershop owner and a sales representative (sales rep) at Hermosa Beauty Supply. Mark the following statements as true (T) or false (F).**

1 __ The man does not currently own any beard trimmers.

2 __ The woman tells the man about a new monogramming service.

3 __ The man places an order for only one type of product.

7 🎧 **Listen again and complete the conversation.**

Owner:	I need new **1** _____ trimmers for my barbershop. They keep getting blunt.
Sales Rep:	You don't need to worry about that with our beard trimmers. They have **2** _____ - _____ _____ and come with a lifetime guarantee.
Owner:	That's impressive.
Sales Rep:	Are there any other **3** _____ you're looking to upgrade?
Owner:	Maybe. I checked out your website and saw that you carry monogrammed **4** _____ _____.
Sales Rep:	We sure do. They've proved very popular.
Owner:	Do you monogram any other products?
Sales Rep:	Actually, we just began offering monogrammed **5** _____ _____.
Owner:	Okay, I'll think about the monogramming. I just want to order the beard **6** _____ today.
Sales Rep:	I'll be happy to help you with that. How many beard trimmers would you like?
Owner:	For now, I'll take five.
Sales Rep:	No problem. Let me start that order for you.

Speaking

8 **With a partner, act out the roles below based on Task 7. Then, switch roles.**

USE LANGUAGE SUCH AS:

I need …

Are there any other products you're looking to …?

I just want to order …

Student A: You are a barbershop owner interested in Hermosa Beauty Supply products. Talk to Student B about:

● which product you are interested in buying (choose at least 2)

● the features of that product

Then, tell Student B which item you want to place an order for.

Student B: You are a sales representative for Hermosa Beauty Supply. Find out which product Student A is interested in buying. Then, respond to Student A's questions.

Writing

9 **You are a barbershop owner who bought some grooming products from Hermosa Beauty Supply. Use the letter and the conversation from Task 8 to write a review of the products on a web page. Include:**

● What product you purchased

● The features of the product

● Whether you were happy or unhappy with the product's performance.

tiara

Get ready!

❶ Before you read the passage, talk about these questions.

1 What occasions do people dress up for?

2 What are some different ways of styling hair for special occasions?

Reading

❷ Read this pamphlet from a salon. Then, mark the following statements as true (T) or false (F).

1 __ A Chignon will draw attention to a woman's facial features.

2 __ A French Braid is typically considered a fancy hair style.

3 __ A Ponytail is a type of updo.

Vocabulary

❸ Read the sentences and choose the correct meaning of the underlined word.

1 Frances tied a <u>ribbon</u> around her hair to make her style look fancier.

   A a narrow section of hair that is often curled

   B a length of narrow material that is used to tie hair

   C a style that involves holding the hair back in a ball shape

2 On her wedding day, Melody wore a sparkly <u>tiara</u> on her head.

   A a style that involves twisting the hair and fastening to the crown of the head

   B a style that involves twisting three strands of hair close to the head

   C a piece of jewelry that resembles a crown

3 Philip worked as a cashier in an <u>accessory</u> store which sold purses and belts.

   A a look that is very informal, relaxed and usually unusual.

   B an object that makes something more attractive or useful

   C a style that involves tying all of the hair at the back of the head and that resembles a horse's tail

Glam Season

Whether you're going to a wedding, prom or anniversary party, Bella Salon has you covered. No matter the occasion, our hair experts have the answer for you.

Updos
For a classic look, go with a versatile **upswept** style. A **full updo** is perfect for bridal hair while **partial updos** are the perfect choice for the Prom. Check out these updos:

Chignon
Nothing says "elegant" like a timeless **Chignon**. This style emphasizes facial features and works great for women with all types of hair. Add a **tiara** for a feminine touch.

French Twist
For a **bohemian** look, try the reinterpreted **French Twist**. Pull a few **tendrils** of hair loose to create a contemporary version of this style.

Other Styles
French Braid
This everyday style can be **dressed up** by weaving colorful flowers or **accessories** throughout the braid. But remember, this style only works on women with shoulder-length to long hair.

Ponytail
Reinvigorate the **Ponytail** by wrapping a **ribbon** around it. Or wear it high and curl the ends to create a cascading effect.

Let Loose
Loose hair is romantic and youthful, but it must be styled in order to fit the occasion. For a sleek and simple look, turn the ends of the hair under. If you want a trendy look, flip out the ends.

❹ Fill in the blanks with the correct words and phrases: *dressed up*, *partial updo*, *French Braid*, *bohemian*.

1 Kay divided Yolanda's hair into three sections and created a _____ .

2 Alicia _____ her French Braid with some colorful ribbon.

3 This season, _____ styles are in, so many people dress like artists and musicians.

4 Kristen wanted to wear her hair up and down, so she opted for a _____ .

5 🎧 Listen and read the pamphlet from a salon again. Which hairstyle would also be suitable for a day at work?

Listening

6 🎧 Listen to a conversation between a client and a stylist at a salon. Choose the correct answers.

1 Why doesn't the stylist give the woman the style that she originally asks for?

    A it is too informal for the event

    B it does not work with her hair length

    C it will take too long to style

    D it works better on women with short hair

2 What can be inferred about the woman?

    A She has short hair.

    B She is married.

    C She is from France.

    D She has curly hair.

7 🎧 Listen again and complete the conversation.

Stylist:	So, tell me, do you have a **1** _____ _____ in mind?
Client:	Actually, I looked through some magazines and got some ideas.
Stylist:	Oh? What type of **2** _____ are you going for?
Client:	I think I'd like a **3** _____ _____ .
Stylist:	Okay, here's the thing, French Braids are beautiful, but I'm afraid it won't work with your **4** _____ _____ .
Client:	I didn't even think of that.
Stylist:	For a French Braid, you need at least **5** _____ - _____ hair.
Client:	I understand. So, what are my options then?
Stylist:	Can I suggest a(n) **6** _____ ?
Client:	Like what?
Stylist:	Well, I think a French **7** _____ would look beautiful and elegant. And we can pull out some hair to create some **8** _____ around your face.
Client:	That sounds perfect. Let's go with that.

Speaking

8 With a partner, act out the roles below based on Task 7. Then, switch roles.

Student A: You are a stylist at the Bella Salon. Talk to Student B to find out what special event they are attending and what type of style they would like. Then, discuss the following points:

- why the style they want won't work
- your suggestion for a different style

Student B: You are a client at a salon. Tell Student A what event you will be attending and what type of style you want. Then, discuss alternate styles and decide which style you want.

Writing

9 You are going to a special event. Use the pamphlet and the conversation from Task 8 to write a note to give to your stylist about hairstyles you like. Include:

- The event that you will attend
- The hairstyles you are considering
- Which hairstyle you think is best for you

Chignon

partial updo

French Braid

Ponytail

Get ready!

❶ Before you read the passage, talk about these questions.

1 What are some common nail problems?

2 Do you know of any remedies or tips for keeping nails healthy?

Reading

❷ Read the article from a health magazine. Then, fill in the blanks using the correct words and phrases from the word bank.

silk wrap   supplement   treated
repair   topical antifungal

Tape or glue can be used to **1**_____ a broken nail, but a **2**_____ is required to mend a split nail. A vitamin **3**_____ can improve the strength of weak nails. Ingrown toenails should be **4**_____ by disinfecting and soaking feet, unless a fungal infection caused the condition. In that instance, a pill or **5**_____ cream can resolve the issue.

Vocabulary

❸ Read the sentence pair. Choose where the words best fit the blanks.

1 **intact / topical**

Sophie broke her nail but kept it _____ with some tape.

Jennifer applied a(n) _____ antifungal cream to her nail.

2 **nail bed / fungus**

Edward's toenail looked yellow and thick because of _____ .

Natalie damaged her _____ while playing basketball and her whole nail turned purple.

3 **salt bath / ingrown toenail**

Hugo's foot hurt too much to play soccer because he had a(n) _____ .

Alana soaked her feet in a(n) _____ to help fix her nail problem.

vitamin supplement

splitting

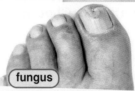
fungus

ingrown toenail

Nail Health

Healthy nails are beautiful nails. The following advice will help you fix the most common nail problems:

Broken Nails
Nails always break or **snag** at the worst times, like when you're at work or in class. For a quick fix, use clear tape to keep the nail **intact**. When you get home, remove any polish and wash the nail. Then, apply nail glue to the break and smooth the nail with an emery board.

Splitting Nails
Splitting can be very painful, especially if it reaches the **nail bed**. When splitting occurs, apply a **silk wrap** to the damaged area. Just be sure to avoid soaking your hands in water, as it will only make the problem worse.

Thin and Brittle Nails
For thin or **brittle** nails, **vitamin supplements** can be the answer. Vitamin B helps with thin nails, and a multivitamin containing calcium, vitamins A, B, C, D and iron can resolve brittle nail issues.

Ingrown Toenails
Ingrown toenails occur when you wear ill-fitting shoes or trim your nails incorrectly. Home remedies include daily soaks in a **salt bath** and disinfecting the area with tea tree oil.

Fungus
Nail **fungus** can make your nails thick and discolored. **Fungal infections** are treated with oral medication or **topical antifungal cream.**

❹ Match the words (1-6) with the definitions (A-F).

1 __ splitting   4 __ silk wrap
2 __ snag   5 __ vitamin supplement
3 __ brittle   6 __ antifungal cream

A an artificial covering that strengthens nails

B to damage by catching on a rough or hard edge

C a medicated lotion that kills fungus

D a pill that contains substances that the body needs in order to stay healthy

E a nail condition in which the nail divides

F weak and easy to break

5 🎧 **Listen and read the article from a health magazine again. What advice does the article give regarding split nails?**

Listening

6 🎧 **Listen to a conversation between a client and a nail technician at a salon. Choose the correct answers.**

1 Why does the woman visit the salon?

    A to request artificial nails

    B to get a pedicure

    C to get help for a nail problem

    D to repair her brittle nails

2 What is true about the woman?

    A She gets regular pedicures.

    B She has had silk wraps in the past.

    C She is not in pain as a result of her condition.

    D She bites her nails.

7 🎧 **Listen again and complete the conversation.**

Client:	Hi, Bill. Boy am I glad to see you!
Nail Technician:	Same here. What can I do for you today, Mrs. Anderson? Just a **1** _____ as usual?
Client:	Actually, I need some help.
Nail Technician:	What's the problem?
Client:	Look at this! My nails are in **2** _____ _____.
Nail Technician:	It looks like you have some **3** _____ _____.
Client:	I noticed them about a week ago, and they've just gotten worse since then.
Nail Technician:	Are they **4** _____?
Client:	Yes, they are.
Nail Technician:	Okay, well don't worry. We'll get them **5** _____ _____.
Client:	How?
Nail Technician:	I'm going to apply **6** _____ _____ _____. Are you familiar with those?
Client:	No, I'm afraid not.
Nail Technician:	They're a type of artificial nail. They help make your **7** _____ _____ stronger. We also use them on people who have brittle nails.
Client:	As long as it makes them better, I'm all for it.

Speaking

8 **With a partner, act out the roles below based on Task 7. Then, switch roles.**

USE LANGUAGE SUCH AS:

Look at this! …

It looks like you have …

Is it painful?

Student A: You are a nail technician at Bella Salon. Find out what nail problem Student B is having. Then, discuss the following:

● whether the condition is painful

● how you will fix the problem

Make sure to explain how your solution works.

Student B: You are a client at the salon. Tell Student A about your nail problem. Then, respond to Student A's question.

Writing

9 **You work in a salon. Use the article and the conversation from Task 8 to write a note to clients about how to avoid nail issues. Include:**

● At least 2 types of nail problems

● How to avoid these problems

21

Your Guide to Artificial Nails

By: Janine Davis

decals

tips

fills

Some people are blessed with perfect nails, but for those of us who have difficulty growing nails, or who are **nail biters**, artificial nails are a guaranteed way to have attractive hands.

Acrylic nails and **tips** are the strongest and most popular type of **artificial** nail. Removal is straightforward and they can easily be **customized** to reflect your personality with **decals**. However, acrylics have some undesirable traits. For instance, they are more likely to damage your natural nails, and they can look fake, unless applied by an expert. Also, you must go back to the salon every 2-3 weeks to get **fills** as your nails grow, so **upkeep** can be expensive.

Gels are a different type of artificial nail. The application process is more pleasant for gels than acrylics because gels are **odorless** and **cure** quickly. They provide a more natural appearance and do not need to be filled as often. However, gels are not without their disadvantages. They cost more and are not as durable as acrylic nails. Furthermore, they must be removed by filing and nail polish isn't always easy to apply.

Get ready!

❶ Before you read the passage, talk about these questions.

1 Do you prefer artificial or natural nails? Why?

2 What are some advantages of artificial nails?

Reading

❷ Read the article from a magazine. Then, choose the right answers.

1 What is the purpose of the article?

   A to explain the benefits and drawbacks of different types of artificial nails

   B to show how to apply fake nails at home

   C to discuss the similarities between acrylics and gels

   D to explain how to maintain artificial nails

2 Which of the following is a difference between acrylic nails and gels?

   A Acrylic nails set faster than gels.

   B Acrylic nails look more authentic than gels.

   C Gels are more likely to harm the natural nail.

   D Gels break more easily than acrylic nails.

3 Why is the long-term cost of acrylics high?

   A They require frequent maintenance.

   B They need to be removed by a professional.

   C The tips must be replaced regularly.

   D The materials used to customize the nails are costly.

Vocabulary

❸ Write a word that is similar in meaning to the underlined part.

1 The elderly couple wanted a house that required minimal cost and effort to maintain. _ p _ e e _

2 Jasmine got rose designs that are applied to the surface of nails because roses are her favorite flowers. _ e _ a _ _

3 Corrine got fake nails that are only attached to the end of the natural nail instead of full acrylics. _ i _ _

4 Laurie's nails never grow very long because she is a person who chews on her nails. _ a _ _ _ _ _ e r

5 Eleanor decided to get a type of artificial nail that is very durable because they were the most affordable option. _ c _ y _ _ c _

❹ Match the words (1-6) with the definitions (A-F).

1 __ cure   4 __ odorless

2 __ artificial   5 __ fills

3 __ customize   6 __ gel

A not real; made to resemble something real or natural

B having no scent

C to make something unique or special

D to prepare for use by placing under a light

E a type of artificial nail that is set by exposing the substance to light

F the application of an artificial nail mixture to new areas of nail growth

5 🎧 **Listen and read the article from a magazine again. What advantages do acrylic nails have over gels?**

Listening

6 🎧 **Listen to a conversation between a client and a nail technician at a salon. Mark the following statements as true (T) or false (F).**

1 __ The client doesn't like the frequent maintenance required by acrylic nails.

2 __ The man only knows how to apply acrylic nails.

3 __ The woman decides to get gel nails.

7 🎧 **Listen again and complete the conversation.**

Client:	What are the advantages of gels?
Nail Technician:	For one, you **1** _____ _____ _____ as often.
Client:	Oh, that sounds great. As much as I enjoy talking to you, I hate having to **2** _____ _____ _____ so often.
Nail Technician:	I understand. Plus, maintenance **3** _____ _____ expensive.
Client:	What are some other advantages?
Nail Technician:	Gels look a lot more **4** _____. That's why so many people prefer them.
Client:	Are there any disadvantages with them?
Nail Technician:	Sure there are. I mean, the **5** _____ does take longer.
Client:	How do you remove them then?
Nail Technician:	You can't just **6** _____ _____ _____. You have to get a professional to file them off. Also, if you break a gel, you can't fix it at home.
Client:	I'd have to come to the salon?
Nail Technician:	Yes, immediately, or you can severely **7** _____ _____ _____ .
Client:	Hmm... I think I'll stick with acrylics.

Speaking

8 **With a partner, act out the roles below based on Task 7. Then, switch roles.**

USE LANGUAGE SUCH AS:

What are the advantages of ...

For one, ...

I think I'll stick with ...

Student A: You are a client at Bella Salon. Tell Student B which type of artificial nails you currently have. Ask Student B questions about:

● the advantages and disadvantages of a different type of artificial nail

Then, tell Student B which kind of artificial nail you want.

Student B: You are a nail technician at Bella Salon. Find out what type of artificial nail Student A has. Then, respond to his or her questions.

Writing

9 **You are a nail technician at a salon. Use the article and the conversation from Task 8 to write a pamphlet about the different types of artificial nails. Include:**

● Reasons to get artificial nails

● Advantages and disadvantages of acrylic nails

● Advantages and disadvantages of gels

(nail biter)

no-smoking policy

disposable gloves

HAZARDOUS WASTE

flammable

Get ready!

1 **Before you read the passage, talk about these questions.**

1 What safety precautions must a beauty salon take?

2 Why is it important to have clean manicure tools?

Reading

2 **Read the letter. Then, mark the following statements as true (T) or false (F).**

1 ___ The salon owner must provide employees with protective equipment.

2 ___ Smoking is not allowed in salons that perform manicures.

3 ___ Salon employees must store tools used during a manicure in a disinfectant solution.

Vocabulary

3 **Read the sentence and choose the correct word.**

1 Max wore a **face mask / UV sanitizer** to avoid breathing in dust at work.

2 The salon has a strict **no-smoking policy / business license** and even staff members must smoke outside of the building.

3 Sally's infection was highly **flammable / communicable** and stopped her from working as a pedicurist.

4 **Read the sentences and choose the correct meaning of the underlined word.**

1 The manicure kit does not include nail polish as we cannot mail <u>flammable</u> materials.

   A capable of transmitting to others easily

   B at a place of business

   C capable of catching fire easily

2 Tina always uses <u>disinfectant</u> to clean her salon's tools.

   A the act of following rules

   B a chemical substance that cleans things and destroys bacteria

   C the act or process of making something clean and healthy

3 The colorist wore <u>disposable gloves</u> to dye her client's hair.

   A hand coverings that can be used and thrown away after use

   B substances that are put on the face to clean the skin

   C gas or vapor that is irritating and often dangerous

Dear Salon Owner,

According to your **business license**, your employees offer **on-site** manicures. There are certain safety and **sanitation** requirements relating to this type of work. Your business must be in **compliance** with the following regulations.

- You must provide your employees with **face masks** and **disposable gloves**.
- Employees must wash their faces, hands and arms frequently.
- Material Safety Data Sheets for all products must be available to employees.
- Your salon must enforce a strict **no-smoking policy** inside, and also near dumpsters that contain **flammable** materials.
- No client with open sores, wounds or infections may have an appointment.
- No employee showing signs of a **communicable** disease may perform services.
- All used equipment must meet disinfection standards. Store all tools in a **UV sanitizer** between uses. Any implements that have come into contact with bodily fluids must be immersed in **disinfectant** solution for ten minutes.
- Clean tools and linens must be used with each new client.
- A constant flow of air must be maintained to prevent the build-up of dangerous **fumes**.

Thank you for your cooperation.

The Department of Workplace Safety

5 🎧 **Listen and read the letter again. What safety rule applies to clients?**

Listening

6 🎧 **Listen to a conversation between a client and a nail technician at a salon. Choose the correct answers.**

1 The client mostly asks questions about _____.

   A protective equipment for employees

   B maintaining her manicure tools at home

   C how to treat a nail infection

   D salon procedures for avoiding the spread of illness

2 What is true about the woman?

   A She is an employee of the Department of Workplace Safety.

   B She is concerned about the risks of infection.

   C She usually gets a manicure and a pedicure at the same time.

   D She brought her own manicure tools to the salon.

7 🎧 **Listen again and complete the conversation.**

Client:	How often do you **1** _____ the equipment?
Nail Technician:	We disinfect all of the tools that we use **2** _____ after the manicure.
Client:	And how exactly are those tools **3** _____?
Nail Technician:	We put them in a disinfectant solution for ten minutes. That's how long the Department of **4** _____ _____ recommends.
Client:	I wonder, do you allow clients to bring their **5** _____ _____ from home?
Nail Technician:	Of course. That's one way to make sure everything is clean.
Client:	I might do that next time.
Nail Technician:	That's not a problem at all. But I assure you, we work very hard to make sure that all of **6** _____ _____ and manicure stations are sanitary. The last thing we want is for our clients to get sick or have a bad experience here.

Speaking

8 **With a partner, act out the roles below based on Task 7. Then, switch roles.**

USE LANGUAGE SUCH AS:

How often do you …

And how exactly are those tools sanitized?

Student A: You are a client having a manicure at a salon. Ask Student B questions about:

● the salon's sanitation procedures

● the salon's policies about bringing manicure tools from home

Student B: You are a nail technician at Bella Salon. Answer Student A's questions and convince him or her that the salon is a safe place to have a manicure.

Writing

9 **You are the owner of a salon. Use the letter and the conversation from Task 8 to write a notice to employees about sanitation. Include:**

● Measures that protect employees

● Measures that protect clients

● The sanitation process at the salon

fair

skin tone

bronzer

makeup counter

There is such a wide variety of makeup products available today that it can be hard to choose the ones that will look best on you. But you can solve this problem learning about your **skin tone** and the **hues** that **complement** it.

Skin Tone

There are two types of skin tone: cool and warm. If you're not sure of your skin tone, there is an easy way to test it. Try on a white blouse and then a cream-colored top. If the white one looks better, you probably have a cool tone, but if the cream-colored one looks better, you likely have a warm tone.

Foundation

Choosing a **foundation** that **matches** your skin tone is essential. Foundations usually have either a blue or yellow **base**. Foundations with blue bases look best with cool skin tones, while yellow-based foundations look best with warm skin tones. For help getting a perfect match, ask a **specialist** at the **makeup counter**.

Blush or Bronzer

Choosing the right **intensity** of **blush** is also crucial. Cool and **fair** skin tones look best with pink or rose-colored blush, while blushes with honey and copper **undertones** will work best with warm and darker skin tones. You may also want to try using **bronzer** instead of blush to give your skin a sun-kissed **glow**.

Get ready!

1 Before you read the passage, talk about these questions.

1 What different types of makeup are available today?

2 What should women consider when choosing a foundation?

Reading

2 Read the article from a fashion magazine. Then, choose the correct answers.

1 What is the article mostly about?
   A how to decide on the right shade of makeup
   B the qualities of different types of foundations
   C where to get help for choosing makeup
   D the reasons that bronzer is better than blush

2 What is the purpose of trying on two different tops?
   A to test the effectiveness of your makeup
   B to tell the difference between warm and cool makeup
   C to determine your skin tone
   D to help you pick out clothes that match your makeup

3 What is probably true about people with cool skin tones?
   A They look best in white clothing.
   B They should use yellow-based foundation.
   C Copper blush suits them.
   D They have dark skin.

Vocabulary

3 Choose the correct word pair to fill in the blanks.

1 Ashley has a warm _____, so she tries to find foundations with a yellow _____ .
   A hue - glow
   B skin tone - base
   C undertone - bronzer

2 The beauty _____ is an expert on all of the products at the _____ .
   A bronzer - base
   B skin tone - hues
   C specialist - makeup counter

3 The _____ has copper and gold _____ and makes warm skin look tanned and youthful.
   A bronzer - undertones
   B hue - bases
   C skin tone - specialists

4 Check (✓) the sentence that uses the underlined part correctly.

1 __ **A** Lisa has <u>fair</u> skin that burns easily in the sun.

__ **B** The <u>intensity</u> of the blush on the young model's face was too glossy.

2 __ **A** Amy <u>complemented</u> her friend's wrong choice of bronzer.

__ **B** The foundation Sue chose didn't <u>match</u> her cool skin tone.

3 __ **A** Hank's skin had a healthy <u>glow</u> after his jog.

__ **B** Brittany put an <u>undertone</u> on before applying her makeup.

5 🎧 Listen and read the article from a fashion magazine again. Which type of foundation would look better on someone with a warm skin tone?

Listening

6 🎧 Listen to a conversation between a customer and a makeup consultant in a store. Mark the following statements as true (T) or false (F).

1 __ The woman has a cool skin tone.

2 __ The woman says that she looks better after applying a foundation with a blue base.

3 __ The makeup consultant recommends a foundation for warm skin tones.

7 🎧 Listen again and complete the conversation.

Client:	I want to try this foundation. Do you have a **1** _____ available?
Makeup consultant:	I do. But I have to say, I don't recommend that one for you, ma'am.
Client:	Why is that?
Makeup consultant:	It wouldn't go with your **2** _____ _____ very well. That foundation is for **3** _____ skin tones.
Client:	To tell you the truth, I've always had trouble finding a foundation that **4** _____ _____ _____. Can you help me find the right one?
Makeup consultant:	I'd be glad to. Now, it looks like you have a cool skin tone, so we need to find a foundation that **5** _____ that.
Client:	What do you mean I have a cool skin tone?
Makeup consultant:	It's one of the two skin tone types.
Client:	I see. So what **6** _____ _____ _____ would go best with my skin tone?
Makeup consultant:	I recommend a foundation with a **7** _____ _____.

Speaking

8 With a partner, act out the roles below based on Task 7. Then, switch roles.

USE LANGUAGE SUCH AS:

Do you have a sample available?

It's one of the two skin tone types.

I recommend a …

Student A: You are a consultant at a makeup counter in a store. Help Student B find the right makeup. First, determine if Student B has a warm or cool skin tone. Based on that information, talk about the following:

● skin tones

● give Student B a recommendation

Student B: You are a customer at a makeup counter. Ask Student A to help you find the right foundation or blush for you. Make sure to ask about:

● foundations

● a recommendation for makeup based on your skin tone

Writing

9 You are an advice columnist for a beauty magazine. Use the article and the conversation from Task 8 to answer a letter from a reader who wants to know more about choosing the correct foundation. Include:

● What type of makeup the reader wants

● How to test for cool or warm skin tones

27

13 Eye makeup techniques

mascara

eye-liner

brow bone

eye shadow

quad

Eye Makeup 101

Eye makeup can create stunning effects when it's properly applied. Use these tips for creating perfect eye makeup every time!

Choose the Right Shades

To make your eyes **stand out**, choose colors that complement your eye color. Use the chart below as a guideline:

Eye color	Complementary Shades
Blue	peach, brown, rust
Green/**hazel**	plum, copper, **metallics**
Brown	gold, blue, green

Tip

Many **cosmetic** companies sell **trios** and **quads** that include shades to suit customers with specific eye colors. These make it very easy to buy shadows that go well with your eyes.

Use a Primer

Have you ever spent half an hour applying your eye shadow only to find that it's gone in a few hours? To avoid this, always use a **primer** before putting on eye makeup.

Blend, Blend, Blend

Most women use at least three different shadows. Blending the different eye shadows you use is the secret to a professional look. Always start by **dusting** a light shadow on the upper part of the lid and along the **brow bone**. Next, apply a medium shade to the eyelid, sweeping the **applicator** from the inside corner of the eye toward the outer edge of the lid. At this point, blend both shades completely. Finally, sweep the darkest color along the **eyelid crease** to add **contours** and dimension to your look.

Get ready!

① Before you read the passage, talk about these questions.

1 What are some different types of eye makeup?

2 How can someone know which eye makeup suits them best?

Reading

② Read the beauty website. Then, mark the following statements as true (T) or false (F).

1 __ Wearing certain shades of eye shadow can make eyes more noticeable.

2 __ Primer helps eye makeup last for a long time.

3 __ The website recommends beginning eye makeup application with the darkest shade of eye shadow.

Vocabulary

③ Match the words (1-6) with the definitions (A-F).

1 __ applicator   3 __ metallic   5 __ quad
2 __ hazel   4 __ primer   6 __ trio

A a color that is a combination of light brown and green

B a product that is applied beneath makeup to help makeup last longer

C a package of eye shadow that includes four different colors

D a special brush or tool that is used for putting a substance on a surface

E a package of eye shadow that includes three different colors

F color that is similar to metals like gold, silver or bronze

④ Fill in the blanks with the correct words and phrases: *dusted, eyelid crease, stand out, brow bone, cosmetics, contours.*

1 Allison wore a bright lipstick to make her lips _____ .

2 Jennifer shaped her eyebrows by plucking the hair that grew along her _____ .

3 The woman _____ her face with a fine white powder.

4 James works for a _____ store that sells lipsticks and mascara.

5 She applied blush along the _____ of her cheeks to make her cheekbones more noticeable.

6 The makeup artist advises using the darkest eye shadow along the _____ .

5 🎧 Listen and read the information from the beauty website again. How can someone make their eye shadow last longer?

Listening

6 🎧 Listen to a conversation between a client and a makeup artist. Answer the questions.

1 What is true about the woman?

    A She looks best in blue eye shadow.

    B She doesn't usually wear makeup.

    C She has blue eyes.

    D She wears a primer.

2 The makeup artist gives the client a sample of _____ .

    A eye shadow

    B primer

    C mascara

    D eye-liner

7 🎧 Listen again and complete the conversation.

Makeup Artist:	Do you like how I used blue eye shadow with brown?
Client:	I can't ever make my eyes **1** _____ _____ like that!
Makeup Artist:	What color eye shadow do you usually use?
Client:	I really like using gray and purple shadows.
Makeup Artist:	Those are nice colors, but they don't really complement blue eyes. You should really **2** _____ _____ brown or rust-colored **3** _____ _____ .
Client:	I didn't realize that made a difference.
Makeup Artist:	Oh, it does. Try the colors I suggested and you'll notice right away.
Client:	Another problem I have is that my eye makeup always **4** _____ _____ after a few hours.
Makeup Artist:	Do you wear a primer?
Client:	No, not usually.
Makeup Artist:	That's your problem. Here's a **5** _____ . Try using it before you apply your eye shadow, eye liner and **6** _____ .
Client:	Thanks, I really appreciate it.

Speaking

8 With a partner, act out the roles below based on Task 7. Then, switch roles.

Student A: You are a makeup artist at Bella Salon. Ask Student B about two of his or her biggest eye makeup problems. Then, talk about:

● the causes of the problem

● how to fix the problem

Student B: You are a client at Bella Salon. Tell Student A about your two biggest eye makeup. Then, ask for suggestions about fixing the problem.

Writing

9 You are a makeup artist. Use the website and the conversation from Task 8 to write a page in a textbook for student makeup artists. Include:

● A common problem with using and applying eye makeup

● How to fix this problem

touch-up kit

wedding party

prom

Special Occasion Makeup

Every woman wants to look beautiful for the most special moments in her life, and the professional makeup artists at Bella Salon are here to make that happen.

Bridal Services

We offer a range of bridal packages that can be individually tailored to each **bride** and her **wedding party**. Each package includes a consultation, a **trial run** and day-of application at the location of the wedding.

We recommend scheduling your bridal makeup appointments several months **in advance** for weddings that take place during the **high season** (May to July). Ask about our discounted rates during the **low season**.

Prom

Make a night to remember with a radiant, professional look. Visit us at the salon or schedule a prom makeup party for you and your friends at your house. Bella Salon also offers specially-priced prom makeup sessions for **parties** over 4. Call today to find out more!

Add Ons:

Touch-up kits **$20**

Contains lipstick, foundation and translucent powder, so you can look beautiful all night!

Airbrush makeup **$100**

Used by professional models and celebrities, this method of makeup application will make you look perfect for all of your photographs.

Makeup Lessons

Did you love the makeup design created by our team on your special day? Do you want to recreate that look at home? **Contract** one of our makeup artists to visit you at home for a **one-on-one** instruction session on how to apply makeup.

Get ready!

1 **Before you read the passage, talk about these questions.**

1   When do people have makeup professionally applied?

2   What are the advantages of getting your makeup professionally done?

Reading

2 **Read this pamphlet from a salon. Then, choose the correct answers.**

1   What is the purpose of the pamphlet?

   A   to give advice for doing professional-looking makeup at home

   B   to explain the advantages of having makeup professionally applied

   C   to describe a number of salon services available for special occasions

   D   to advertise seasonal offers on special occasion packages

2   What is true about the salon's bridal makeup services?

   A   They are in high demand between May and July.

   B   They are not available during the low season.

   C   They take place at the salon's location.

   D   They include a touch-up kit.

3   What is true about the add ons?

   A   They are typically used by people who need to take a lot of photographs.

   B   They are only available for evening events.

   C   They include makeup that is not used by professional models.

   D   They are not included in the price of the bridal or prom packages.

Vocabulary

3 **Read the sentence pair. Choose where the words best fit the blanks.**

1   **trial run / touch-up kit**

   Sara used the items in her _____ to freshen up her makeup after a night of dancing.

   The makeup artist tried different makeup styles on Felicia during the _____ before her wedding.

2   **prom / wedding party**

   The teenage girls had makeup lessons a week before the _____ .

   Jesse thanked the bridal service for making the _____ look so beautiful.

3   **bride / party**

   The _____ wanted airbrush makeup on her special day.

   Karen booked some makeup sessions for a _____ of five.

4   **in advance / one-on-one**

   Karen offers _____ sessions to help her clients learn how to apply makeup.

   The mother of the bride scheduled a makeover at her home well _____ .

4 Write a word that is similar in meaning to the underlined part.

1 According to the fashion magazine, liquid makeup sprayed from an air-operated tool is the latest trend in cosmetics.
_ i _ b _ u s _ _ a _ e _ p

2 Bridal services may be a little more expensive during the busiest time of the year. _ i _ h _ e _ _ o n

3 Alex paid for the temporary services of a photographer to take pictures at his wedding. _ o n _ r a _ t e _

4 It's much easier to get a bridal makeover during the quietest time of the year. _ o _ s _ _ s _ n

5 🎧 Listen and read the pamphlet from a salon again. What must someone do if they want a bridal makeup appointment during the summer?

Listening

6 🎧 Listen to a conversation between a caller and a receptionist at Bella Salon. Mark the following statements as true (T) or false (F).

1 _ The caller wants to find out about bridal makeup.

2 _ The caller is interested in an add on service.

3 _ The makeup artist will do the woman's bridal makeup in the salon.

7 🎧 Listen again and complete the conversation.

Caller:	Hello, I'm interested in **1** _____ _____ .
Receptionist:	Do you want our **2** _____ _____ just for yourself?
Caller:	No, I want to include the **3** _____ _____ _____ . It's going to be six of us in all.
Receptionist:	That's not a problem. Most of our **4** _____ _____ are designed for parties of four or more.
Caller:	So, how does it work? Do we visit the salon for the makeup?
Receptionist:	No. The makeup artist will go out to the **5** _____ of the wedding.
Caller:	Oh, great. I didn't want to go across town for my makeup on my **6** _____ _____ .
Receptionist:	Of course not. On that day, you'll have enough to worry about.
Caller:	There's just one more thing - I'll be in a lot of pictures that day and I heard that **7** _____ _____ photographs really well. Do you offer that?
Receptionist:	We sure do.

Speaking

8 With a partner, act out the roles below based on Task 7. Then, switch roles.

Student A: You are a caller who wants more information about special occasion makeup services at Bella Salon. Tell Student B whether you are planning for a wedding or a prom and how many people you need makeup service for. Then, ask about:

● where the makeup application takes places

● whether the salon offers an add on service

Student B: You are the receptionist at Bella Salon. Ask Student A how many people he or she needs makeup service for. Then, answer his or her questions.

Writing

9 You are a salon owner. Use the pamphlet and the conversation in Task 8 to write about a booking that you have received. Include:

● What special event the package is for

● How many people are included in the package

● What other services are required

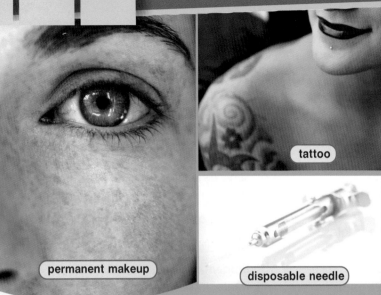

permanent makeup

tattoo

disposable needle

practitioner

Is Permanent Makeup Right for Me?

Many of our clients have expressed interest in **permanent makeup**. While such procedures are not performed at Bella Salon, we are happy to **refer** you to **reputable** and **qualified** permanent makeup **practitioners**.

What is permanent makeup?

Permanent makeup is created by **tattooing** the skin to give the appearance of makeup. Eyeliner, lip liner, lip color and eyebrows are some of the most common permanent cosmetic procedures.

Pros

It's convenient, you always leave the house wearing professional-looking makeup. And you can forget about lipstick that **bleeds** or smudged eye shadow! Your makeup will always stay where it's supposed to. It's **waterproof** and sweat-proof. A rainstorm or physical activity will never ruin your look again!

Cons

It limits your ability to change your appearance. What appeals to you now may not be age appropriate later. The procedures can be painful and there is the possibility of infection.

Tips for Permanent Makeup

Before the Procedure

Make sure that the **practitioner** uses **disposable needles**. Clear your schedule for several days, to give the **swelling** time to go down.

After the procedure

Do not panic if your makeup is the wrong color for 2-3 days after the procedure. It takes that long for excess **pigment** to shed.

Ask at the front desk for more information on permanent makeup.

Get ready!

❶ **Before you read the passage, talk about these questions.**

1   Would you consider having permanent makeup?

2   What are the benefits of permanent makeup?

Reading

❷ **Read the pamphlet. Then, choose the correct answers.**

1   What is the pamphlet mostly about?
   A   the qualifications of the permanent makeup practitioners at Bella Salon
   B   general information about getting permanent makeup
   C   a comparison of permanent makeup and traditional makeup
   D   the areas of the face best suited for permanent makeup application

2   According to the pamphlet, what is a disadvantage of permanent makeup?
   A   Application might be painful.
   B   It is not age appropriate.
   C   It makes people look older.
   D   It usually leads to illness.

3   What is probably true about people with permanent makeup?
   A   They change their looks often.
   B   They do a lot of physical activities.
   C   They don't have to worry about daily makeup application.
   D   They don't dress appropriately for their age.

Vocabulary

❸ **Read the sentence and choose the correct word.**

1   My masseur **referred / tattooed** me to a well-known permanent makeup practitioner.

2   With a degree and twenty years of experience, the manicurist was highly **qualified / reputable** for the job.

3   After having a tattoo, Randy put ointment on it to reduce the **pigment / swelling**.

4   Eunice decided to get **permanent makeup / disposable needles** so she wouldn't have to apply lipstick every day.

5   Shawn is a **reputable / waterproof** practitioner in his neighborhood.

4 Match the words (1-6) with the definitions (A-F).

1 __ tattoo   4 __ bleed

2 __ pigment   5 __ practitioner

3 __ disposable needle   6 __ reputable

A a person who works in a specific profession or who does a specific activity

B to create a permanent design by applying colored inks under the skin

C to spread to another area

D known by others to be good and honest

E a very thin, metal tube that punctures the skin and is thrown away after one use

F a substance used to change the color of something

5 🎧 Listen and read the pamphlet again. Why would someone consider permanent makeup?

Listening

6 🎧 Listen to a conversation between a client and a permanent makeup consultant. Mark the statements as true (T) or false (F).

1 __ The woman wants to get permanent makeup on her lips.

2 __ The woman is concerned about the procedure being painful.

3 __ The consultant says permanent makeup only lasts for four days.

7 🎧 Listen again and complete the conversation.

Consultant:	First, where do you want the **1** _____ _____ ?
Client:	I was thinking about getting my **2** _____ done.
Consultant:	The eyebrows are actually one of the most **3** _____ _____ we do, along with the lips.
Client:	My question is, does it hurt?
Consultant:	To be honest, the procedure is slighty **4** _____ . But the pain is manageable.
Client:	Okay. I can deal with a little pain.
Consultant:	Do you have any other questions?
Client:	Yes, I'm wondering about the **5** _____ _____ .
Consultant:	Okay, this is important, you need at least four days to recover.
Client:	Four days! That seems like a long time.
Consultant:	Also, after the procedure, you'll experience **6** _____ _____ .
Client:	And it takes four days for the swelling to go down?
Consultant:	That's right.

Speaking

8 With a partner, act out the roles below based on Task 7. Then, switch roles.

USE LANGUAGE SUCH AS:

First, where do you want the permanent makeup?

My question is, does it hurt?

Yes, I'm wondering about the recovery time.

Student A: You are a consultant for a permanent makeup practitioner. Find out where Student B wants permanent makeup. Then, answer his or her questions about the procedure.

Student B: You are a client who is thinking about getting permanent makeup. Tell Student A where you want permanent makeup. Then, ask about:

● whether the procedure hurts

● the recovery time

Based on the information that Student A gives you, make a decision about whether you will get permanent makeup. Explain your decision.

Writing

9 You are a consultant for a permanent makeup practitioner. Use the pamphlet and the conversation in Task 8 to write a note about a recent consultation. Include:

● What type of permanent makeup the client was interested in

● What questions the client had and how you answered them

absorb [V-I & T-U5] To **absorb** something is to soak something up, especially liquid.

accessory [N-COUNT-U8] An **accessory** is an object that makes something more attractive or useful. Handbags, belts and earrings are examples of accessories.

acrylic nail [N-COUNT or UNCOUNT-U10] **Acrylic nails** are a very strong type of fake nail.

air dry [V-I & T-U5] To **air dry** hair is to let hair dry without using a blow dryer.

airbrush makeup [N-UNCOUNT-U14] **Airbrush makeup** is liquid makeup that is sprayed onto the face using an air-operated tool, similar to those used to paint cars.

allergic reaction [N-COUNT-U3] An **allergic reaction** is a medical condition that causes skin to grow red and sore or a person to become ill. This is a result of a strong intolerance to something and can be life-threatening.

antifungal cream [N-UNCOUNT-U9] **Antifungal cream** is a medicated lotion that reduces the amount of fungi on the skin to normal levels.

applicator [N-COUNT-U13] An **applicator** is a special brush or tool that is used for applying a substance on the surface of something.

apply to [V-I+to-U1] To **apply to** someone is to affect or relate to someone.

artificial [ADJ-U10] If something is **artificial**, it is something not real made to resemble something real or natural.

base [N-COUNT-U12] A **base** is the primary part of something.

base color [N-COUNT-U4] **Base color** is the natural color of hair before it is altered with dye.

beard trimmer [N-COUNT-U7] A **beard trimmer** is a device designed to trim, groom and shape facial hair.

bill [N-COUNT-U2] A **bill** is a document which details the cost of services or goods provided to the customer.

blade [N-COUNT-U7] A **blade** is the sharp, flat part of a tool, knife or razor that is used for cutting.

bleach [V-T-U4] To **bleach** is to remove color from something, particularly by using chemicals.

bleed [V-I-U15] To **bleed** is to spread over a wide area.

blow-dry [N-UNCOUNT U1] A **blow-dry** is a method of drying hair using a blow dryer.

blush [N-COUNT or UNCOUNT-U12] A **blush** is a powder or cream applied on cheeks to give them color.

bohemian [ADJ-U8] If something is **bohemian**, it is relaxed and informal.

botched [ADJ-U4] If something is **botched**, it is spoiled by a mistake.

bride [N-COUNT-U14] A **bride** is a woman who is getting married.

brittle [ADJ-U9] If something is **brittle**, it is weak and easy to break.

bronzer [N-UNCOUNT-U12] **Bronzer** is a cosmetic product intended to give the appearance of having a tan.

brow bone [N-COUNT-U13] The **brow bone** is the bony ridge beneath the eyebrow.

buildup [N-UNCOUNT-U6] **Buildup** is the collection of residue from styling products which can make hair hard to style and manage.

business license [N-COUNT-U11] A **business license** is an official document that allows a person to operate a business.

cap highlight [N-COUNT-U4] A **cap highlight** is a highlighting method that involves pulling sections of hair through a cap so that it can be colored.

cash [N-UNCOUNT-U2] **Cash** is money that is made up of bills and coins.

Chignon [N-COUNT-U8] A **chignon** is a hairstyle in which a woman's hair is held back in a ball on the back of her head.

clarifying shampoo [N-UNCOUNT-U6] **Clarifying shampoo** is a type of cleansing product for hair which removes the residue from styling products.

close shave [N PHRASE-U7] A **close shave** is a shave that removes all hair and leaves skin completely smooth.

communicable [ADJ-U11] If something is **communicable**, it can be transmitted from one person or animal to another very easily.

complement [V-T-U12] To **complement** something is to make it better when combined with something else.

compliance [N-UNCOUNT-U11] To be in **compliance** with something is to be going according to a rule or regulation.

complimentary [ADJ-U1] If something is **complimentary**, it is free.

conceal [V-T-U3] To **conceal** something is to hide it.

conditioner [N-UNCOUNT-U6] **Conditioner** is a liquid solution applied to hair after shampooing to soften and improve the quality of the hair.

contour [N-COUNT-U13] A **contour** is a noticeable shape to the outside edges or surface of something.

contract [V-T-U14] To **contract** is to hire someone to do a job.

corrective [ADJ-U4] If something is **corrective**, it is able or intended to fix something.

cosmetics [N-UNCOUNT-U13] **Cosmetics** are beauty products that help improve a person's appearance.

coupon [N-COUNT-U2] A **coupon** is a piece of paper issued by a store that gives customers an offer, such as a discount.

credit card [N-COUNT-U2] A **credit card** is a plastic card that customers use to buy goods or services and pay for them later.

cure [V-T-U10] To **cure** is to use a special process (such as exposure to light) to prepare artificial nails for use.

curl pattern [N-COUNT-U5] A **curl pattern** is the distinctive shape of curls.

customize [V-T-U10] To **customize** is to alter something so that it is exactly what a person wants. This often involves changing the appearance of something to make it look special or unique.

damage [V-T-U3] To **damage** something is to harm it.

damp [ADJ-U5] If something is **damp**, it is slightly wet.

debit card [N-COUNT-U2] A **debit card** is a plastic card that takes money directly from a person's bank account to pay for goods.

decal [N-COUNT-U10] A **decal** is a design that is often applied to the surface of nails.

diffuser [N-COUNT-U5] A **diffuser** is a bell-shaped object that attaches to a standard blow dryer. It reduces the amount of air flow coming from a blow dryer and helps prevent frizz.

discount [N-COUNT-U1] A **discount** is a decrease in the price of something.

disinfectant [N-COUNT or UNCOUNT-U11] **Disinfectant** is a chemical substance that destroys bacteria and makes things extremely clean.

disposable glove [N-COUNT-U11] A **disposable glove** is a glove that is worn for protection when handling chemicals and then thrown out after one use.

disposable needle [N-COUNT-U15] A **disposable needle** is a thin, metal tube that punctures the skin and that is thrown away after one use.

double process color [N-UNCOUNT-U4] **Double process color** is a coloring technique that involves bleaching the hair first then adding the desired color. It is typically used when lightening hair.

dress up [PHRASAL V-U8] To **dress up** is to make the appearance of something more formal than usual.

dry cut [N-COUNT-U5] A **dry cut** is a method of cutting curly hair that involves cutting while the hair is dry, so the stylist can work better with the client's curl pattern.

dust [V-T-U13] To **dust** something is to apply a thin coat of powder to something.

electric razor [N-COUNT-U7] An **electric razor** is a men's hair removal device with several blades which rolls backwards and forwards on the skin.

enhance [V-T-U5] To **enhance** is to improve how something looks or feels as well as its quality.

eyelid crease [N-COUNT/UNCOUNT-U13] An **eyelid crease** is the folding line of the eye socket.

expire [V-I-U2] To **expire** is to no longer be usable.

eye-liner [N-UNCOUNT-U13] An **eye-liner** is a special pencil that is used to emphasize the edges around a person's eyes.

Glossary

eye shadow [N-UNCOUNT-U13] Eye shadow is a type of powder or cream that is used to add color to a person's upper eyelids.

face mask [N-COUNT-U11] A face mask (or dust mask) is something that covers the face in order to protect it.

fade [V-I-U3] To fade is to grow paler and lose coloring.

fair [ADJ-U12] If something is fair, it is light colored.

featured product [N PHRASE-U1] A featured product is an item that a store presents as a special attraction.

fill [N-COUNT-U10] A fill is a process in which the gap between the cuticle and the artificial nail is filled in and any necessary repairs to the nail are made.

film [N-COUNT-U6] A film is a thin covering.

flammable [ADJ-U11] If something is flammable, it burns easily and fast.

foil highlight [N-COUNT-U4] A foil highlight is a highlighting method that involves wrapping sections of hair in foil so that they can be colored. It allows colorists to color each section a different color.

foundation [N-UNCOUNT-U12] Foundation is a kind of makeup that is applied to the skin before other makeup is applied.

fragrance-free [ADJ-U6] If something is fragrance-free, it doesn't have a smell.

frayed [ADJ-U5] If something is frayed, it is worn out or shredded.

French Braid [N-COUNT-U8] A French Braid is a hairstyle that involves dividing the hair into three sections and weaving it together, slowly drawing more hair into the braid until all the hair is included.

French Twist [N-COUNT-U8] A French Twist is a hairstyle that involves twisting the hair up, tucking in the ends and fastening it against the head.

full updo [N PHRASE-U8] A full updo is a hairstyle in which all the hair is gathered on the top of the head.

fumes [N-UNCOUNT-U11] Fumes are gases or vapor that cause irritation and are often dangerous when inhaled.

fungal infection [N-COUNT-U9] A fungal infection is an inflammatory condition caused by fungus.

fungus [N-UNCOUNT-U9] Fungus is any of a group of organisms that feed on organic matter.

gel [N-UNCOUNT-U6] Gel is a clear, thick liquid substance used to style hair.

gels [N-COUNT or UNCOUNT-U10] Gels are a very realistic and flexible type of artificial nails.

gift certificate [N-COUNT-U2] A gift certificate is a document issued from a business that is worth a certain sum of money for goods or services offered at that business.

glow [N-COUNT-U12] A glow is the state of emitting light.

grooming [N-UNCOUNT-U7] Grooming is the process of cleaning and tidying someone.

grow out [V-PHRASE-U3] To grow out is to let hair grow until its previous color or style is no longer visible.

hair gel [N-UNCOUNT-U6] Hair gel is a thick, spreadable hair product that holds hair in place.

hairspray [N-UNCOUNT-U6] Hairspray is a sticky substance that is usually sprayed from an aerosol can onto hair in order to hold it in place.

hazel [ADJ-U13] If eyes are hazel, they are a combination of light brown and green.

high season [N-UNCOUNT-U14] High season is a time of the year when people do the most of an activity like travelling or getting married. Prices are usually higher during high season.

highlights [N-UNCOUNT-U4] Highlights are sections of hair that are a lighter color than the rest.

home hair color kit [N-COUNT-U4] A home hair color kit is a package that contains all of the items needed to dye hair at home.

hue [N-COUNT-U12] A hue is the degree of lightness, darkness or strength of a color.

humidity [N-UNCOUNT-U5] Humidity is the quantity of water contained in the air.

in advance [phr-U14] To do something in advance is to do it prior to a certain time or date.

ingrown toenail [N-COUNT-U9] An **ingrown toenail** is a condition in which the edges or tip of the nail grow into the skin.

intact [ADJ-U9] If something is **intact**, it is not harmed, spoiled or broken.

intensity [N-UNCOUNT-U12] **Intensity** is the strength of something that can be measured, such as light.

lighten [V-I or T-U3] To **lighten** something is to make it brighter or less dark.

lightweight [ADJ-U6] If something is **lightweight**, it is not powerful or it is the opposite of heavy duty.

loose hair [N PHRASE-U8] **Loose hair** describes hair which is styled without being tied up or back.

low season [N-UNCOUNT-U14] **Low season** is a time of the year when few people travel or get married. Prices are usually lower during low season.

lowlights [N-UNCOUNT-U4] **Lowlights** are sections of hair that are a darker color than the rest.

makeup counter [N-COUNT-U12] A **makeup counter** is a place in a store where cosmetics are sold.

manageable [ADJ-U5] If something is **manageable**, it is easy to take care of.

mascara [N-UNCOUNT-U13] A **mascara** is a substance used as makeup to darken or lengthen a person's eyelashes.

match [V-T-U12] To **match** something is to become equal or the same as something.

metallic [ADJ-U13] If something is **metallic**, it has the same color of metals like gold, silver or bronze.

method of payment [N-COUNT-U2] A **method of payment** is a way of giving a person or business money that is owed.

mild [ADJ-U6] If something is **mild**, it is gentle and unlikely to cause side effects.

mousse [N-UNCOUNT-U6] **Mousse** is a foamy hair product that is used to style hair or make it appear thicker.

mustache care [N PHRASE-U7] **Mustache care** is the styling and trimming of the facial hair on a man's upper lip.

mustache scissors [N-UNCOUNT-U7] **Mustache scissors** are used to trim the hair of a mustache.

mustache wax [N-UNCOUNT-U7] **Mustache wax** is a sticky substance used to make mustache hair stay in place.

nail bed [N-COUNT-U9] The **nail bed** is the area under a fingernail.

nail biter [N-COUNT-U10] A **nail biter** is a person who bites or chews on their fingernails or the skin surrounding the nail, especially when stressed or nervous.

nose and ear hair trimmer [N-COUNT-U7] A **nose and ear hair trimmer** is a tool used for removing unwanted hair from the ears or nose.

no-smoking policy [N-COUNT-U11] A **no-smoking policy** is a rule that does not allow smoking in a place.

nourish [V-T-U6] To **nourish** something is to provide it with the substances and care needed to survive, grow and be healthy.

odorless [ADJ-U10] If something is **odorless**, it has no scent.

one-on-one [N-UNCOUNT-U14] If something happens **one-on-one** it occurs between two people.

on-site [ADJ-U11] If something occurs **on-site**, it happens in that place.

package [N-COUNT-U1] A **package** is a group of services or items sold together for one (often reduced) price.

palette [N-COUNT-U3] A **palette** is the range of colors available for a specific purpose.

partial updo [N-COUNT-U8] A **partial updo** is a hairstyle that involves sweeping the top section of the hair away from the face and piling it on top of the head.

party [N-COUNT-U14] A **party** is a group of people taking part in the same activity.

patch test [N-COUNT-U3] A **patch test** involves applying a small amount of a substance to someone in order to check for an allergic reaction.

payment procedure [N-COUNT-U2] A **payment procedure** is the typical or correct way of paying for something.

permanent [ADJ-U3] If something is **permanent**, it continues or happens for a long time.

Glossary

permanent makeup [N-UNCOUNT-U15] **Permanent makeup** is a type of cosmetic that is applied by tattooing ink under the skin in order to enhance a person's appearance.

personal check [N-COUNT-U2] A **personal check** is a piece of printed paper which someone's fills in an amount of money to pay for things and the bank then debits this amount from the person's account.

pigment [N-COUNT or UNCOUNT-U15] **Pigment** is a substance that is used to change the color of something.

pomade [N-UNCOUNT-U6] **Pomade** is a waxy substance that is used to smooth and care for hair.

ponytail [N-COUNT-U8] A **ponytail** is a hairstyle that involves tying all of the hair at the back of the head and resembles a horse's tail.

practitioner [N-COUNT-U15] A **practitioner** is a person who works in a specific profession or who performs a specific activity.

pricing [N-UNCOUNT-U1] **Pricing** is the set cost for services or goods at a business.

primer [N-COUNT-U13] A **primer** is a cosmetic product that is applied beneath eye shadow in order to help the eye shadow last longer.

prom [N-COUNT-U14] A **prom** is a formal party with dancing for senior students at the end of the year.

promotion [N-COUNT-U1] A **promotion** is a set of activities or products that bring attention and increased sales to a business.

quad [N-COUNT-U13] A **quad** is a package of eye shadows that includes four different colors.

qualified [ADJ-U15] If a person is **qualified**, he or she has the appropriate skills, knowledge or training for a specific job.

range from [V-T+PREP-U1] To **range from** is to have a lower and upper limit in an amount or number of sth offered.

reduced rate [N PHRASE-U1] A **reduced rate** is a price for something that is lower than the usual price.

refer [V-T-U15] To **refer** is to send someone or something to another person, place or organization, in order to receive information, help or guidance.

refund [V-T-U2] To **refund** money is to return a person's money because they do not want or are dissatisfied with a product or service.

rejuvenation [N-UNCOUNT-U1] **Rejuvenation** is when someone has been made to feel young and strong again.

repel [V-T-U5] To **repel** something is to force it to go away.

reputable [ADJ-U15] If someone is **reputable**, he or she is known by others to be good and honest.

retouch [V-T-U3] To **retouch** is to make minor alterations to something. When referring to hair, it means to re-dye the roots of the hair.

ribbon [N-COUNT or UNCOUNT-U8] A **ribbon** is a length of narrow material that is used to tie women's hair.

salt bath [N-COUNT-U9] A **salt bath** is a container containing a mixture of water and salt. It is often used as a remedy for a number of ailments.

sanitation [N-UNCOUNT-U11] **Sanitation** is the conditions and processes connected to people's health.

scrunch [V-I/T-U5] To **scrunch** hair is to squeeze it in the palm of your hand.

seasonal [ADJ-U1] If something is **seasonal**, it is only available during a specific time of the year.

self-sharpening blade [N-COUNT-U7] A **self-sharpening blade** is a blade that keeps itself sharp and able to cut.

semi-permanent [ADJ-U3] If something is **semi-permanent**, it lasts for a period of time, but not for longer.

shampoo [N-UNCOUNT-U6] **Shampoo** is a special washing liquid for hair.

shaving bowl [N-COUNT-U7] A **shaving bowl** is a wide, round container that is open at the top and is used for lathering shaving cream.

shaving brush [N-COUNT-U7] A **shaving brush** is a small brush made of hair or bristles and attached to a handle that is used to apply shaving cream or soap to a man's face.

sideburns [N-UNCOUNT-U7] **Sideburns** are patches of hair that grow down the side of a man's face.

silicone [N-UNCOUNT-U5] **Silicone** is a water and heat-resistant substance.

silk wrap [N-COUNT or UNCOUNT-U9] A **silk wrap** is a type of artificial nail which is intended to make the natural nail stronger and more attractive. Pieces of silk fabric are cut to size, then applied to the natural nail with a sealant.

single process color [N-UNCOUNT-U4] **Single process color** is a coloring technique that involves coloring all of the hair one color.

skin tone [N-UNCOUNT-U12] **Skin tone** is the color of a person's skin.

snag [V-I or T-U9] To **snag** is to damage something by getting it stuck on something rough or sharp.

special [N-COUNT-U1] A **special** is an offering of a product or service, usually at a reduced price.

specialist [N-COUNT-U12] A **specialist** is a person who is an expert at one occupation.

splitting [N-UNCOUNT-U9] **Splitting** is a nail condition in which the nail develops a vertical division.

spritz [N-COUNT-U6] A **spritz** is a liquid hair product that is sprayed over hair in order to hold it in place.

stand out [PHRASAL V-U13] To **stand out** is to be distinctive and get attention.

start at [V-I-U1] To **start at** is to be the lowest point or price of something.

straight razor [N-COUNT-U7] A **straight razor** is a traditional razor with a long blade that folds out from a handle.

strop [N-COUNT-U7] A **strop** is a narrow piece of leather used for keeping a razor sharp.

swelling [N-UNCOUNT-U15] **Swelling** is the process of expansion as a result of illness or injury; to become puffed up.

tattoo [V-T-U15] To **tattoo** is to create a permanent design by applying colored inks under the skin.

tax [N-COUNT-U2] A **tax** is money that the government charges the citizens of a place in order to pay for services for the public.

tendrils [N-COUNT-U8] **Tendrils** are thin sections of hair that are curled.

test solution [N-COUNT-U3] A **test solution** is a combination of chemicals that will be used later in larger amounts if it is proven to be safe.

tiara [N-COUNT-U8] A **tiara** is a piece of jewelry that resembles a crown and is worn during formal events.

tip [N-COUNT-U10] A **tip** is a type of artificial nail that is only attached to the end of the nail and does not cover the entire nail.

tip [N-COUNT-U2] A **tip** is a small amount of extra money that customers give to a person who provides good service.

topical [ADJ-U9] If something is **topical**, it is used on, or associated with, a particular part of the body.

touch-up kit [N-COUNT-U14] A **touch-up kit** is a small bag of cosmetics used to slightly improve, change or add something.

trial run [N-COUNT-U14] A **trial run** is an occasion when you test a new method or system to see if it works or goes well.

trio [N-COUNT-U13] A **trio** is a package of eye shadows that includes three different colors.

two-tone [ADJ-U4] **Two-tone** hair is hair that has two very different colors in it.

undertone [N-COUNT-U12] An **undertone** is a color that is seen through a second color and that slightly alters the appearance of that second color.

upkeep [N-UNCOUNT-U10] **Upkeep** is the process or cost of maintaining something or of keeping something in good condition.

upswept [ADJ-U8] If hair is **upswept**, it is smoothed or combed upwards in the back, and piled on top of a woman's head.

UV sanitizer [N-COUNT-U11] A **UV sanitizer** is a machine that uses UV rays (a type of light) to kill germs and bacteria.

valid [ADJ-U2] A certificate or document is **valid** when it is used within a set time limit.

vitamin supplement [N-COUNT-U9] A **vitamin supplement** is a pill that contains the natural substances that the body needs in order to stay healthy.

waterproof [ADJ-U15] If something is **waterproof**, it is able to resist water or does not get damaged by water.

wedding party [N-COUNT-U14] A **wedding party** is made up of the bride and groom, their parents and all male and female attendants.

Career Paths

English for Specific Purposes

http://www.expresspublishing.co.uk

The ideal series to help professionals and students develop the language skills they need to succeed in a professional work situation

Engineering

Information Technology

Business English

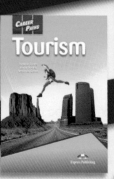
Tourism

Hotels & Catering

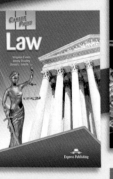
Law

Beauty Salon

Accounting

Nursing

Secretarial

Agriculture

Banking

Environmental Science

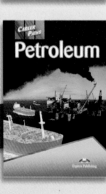
Petroleum

Medical

Electronics

Finance

Civil Aviation

Merchant Navy

Mechanics

Command & Control

Air Force

Police

Navy

Express Publishing